IDENTIFICATION GUIDES

European Insects

Publisher and Creative Director: Nick Wells
Project Editor: Sara Robson
Picture Research: Gemma Walters
Consultant Naturalist: Chris McLaren
Art Director: Mike Spender
Digital Design and Production: Chris Herbert
Layout Design: Lucy Robins

Special thanks to: Chelsea Edwards, Julie Pallot, Helen Tovey and Claire Walker

11 10

3 5 7 9 10 8 6 4 2

This edition first published 2007 by
FLAME TREE PUBLISHING
Crabtree Hall, Crabtree Lane
Fulham, London SW6 6TY
United Kingdom

www.flametreepublishing.com

Flame Tree Publishing is part of the Foundry Creative Media Co. Ltd.

ISBN 978-1-84451-920-0

A CIP record for this book is available from the British Library upon request.

Printed in China

IDENTIFICATION GUIDES

European Insects

Pamela Forey and Cecilia Fitzsimons

FLAME TREE
PUBLISHING

Contents

Introduction

There are about 20,000 known species of insects in the British Isles and over a million in the world, by far the largest single biological group in this country or in the whole world. They are enormously important in the impact that they have on the environment; they pollinate the flowers of many wild plants and trees as well as crops and fruits, so that without them those crops would not set seed; others we class as pests since they eat the leaves, fruits and roots of wild plants, crops and trees, causing great destruction and high economic losses; more subtly, many others act as regulators of the pests, since they prey on them, parasitize them and keep their populations under control; yet others carry diseases like malaria and typhoid. A world without insects is unimaginable; they occupy crucial positions in every habitat in the land and play key roles in supporting and maintaining the present balance of nature.

Whole libraries are devoted solely to insects and a book of this size cannot provide anything but an introduction to them, a hint of their diversity and form. However, it will enable the reader to identify many of the major insect families and to allocate many insects to their proper place within the group as a whole. Thus, with this book, the reader will be able first to identify an insect as a beetle, for example, and then to decide that it is a leaf beetle, belonging to the leaf beetle family.

How to Use this Book

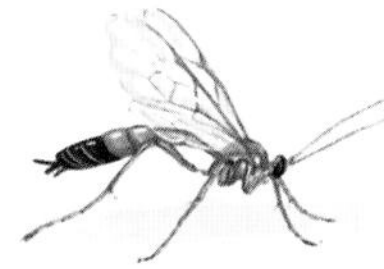

We have divided the book into sections based mainly on the biology of the insects themselves; however we have grouped the many smaller groups of insects like springtails, mayflies, lacewings, etc. together in a section at the end, even though they are unrelated to each other. The sections are **Butterflies and Moths; Bees, Wasps and Ants; Flies; Beetles; Bugs; Homopteran Bugs; Grasshoppers and Crickets; Other Insects**. If you are confident that you can identify an insect, as a beetle or butterfly for example, you will be able to turn directly to the section on beetles or butterflies to identify it more accurately. If however, you are unsure of the major group to which it belongs then you can use the key in the **Guide to Identification**, which follows on the next page, to find the right section.

Guide to Identification

Insects are distinguished from all other animals by the following features: they have bodies with hard exoskeletons, divided into three sections (head, thorax and abdomen); there are two antennae on the head; and three pairs of legs and two pairs of wings on the thorax.

In this guide we have used the differences in the wings of the various groups of insects to enable you to identify the group to which any insect belongs. Page numbers given at the end of each category will enable you to turn quickly to the relevant section.

Wingless insects

Very primitive insects, together with some others, never have wings at any time of their lives. These include the primitive Springtails and Silverfish (p.344, p.346) and the Fleas and Lice (p.342–43). Other insects have wingless forms as well as winged individuals; these include Ants (p.126), which have wingless workers in the nest; some Earwigs (p.332) are wingless, as are some crickets and beetles; females of Oriental Cockroaches (p.312) are wingless as are glow-worms (p.256) and some moths.

Insects in which the fore wings are different to the hind wings

In several groups of insects the fore wings are hardened and strengthened while the hind wings, which are the wings used for flight, are membranous. When the insect is on the ground or at rest, the delicate hind wings are covered and protected by the fore wings. In Grasshoppers (p.298–311) and Cockroaches (p.312) the fore wings are long and narrow, and although they are thickened and leathery they still retain veins. Their hind wings are folded like fans under the fore wings when not in use. Earwigs (p.332) have very short leathery fore wings and the membranous hind wings are folded like fans beneath them. Mantises (p.337) also have leathery, thickened fore wings. In Bugs (p.262–87) the base of each fore wing is leathery and often coloured while the tip is membranous. Some homopteran bugs (p.288, p.294–96) have uniformly thickened fore wings. In Beetles (p.180–261) the fore wings are veinless, very tough or even hard, and they meet in a straight line down the centre of the back.

Insects which have two pairs of membranous wings

Several groups of insects have two similar pairs of membranous wings. These include some Homopteran Bugs (p.288–92), Lacewings (p.314), Dragonflies, Damselflies, Stoneflies and Mayflies (p.320–30), Ant-Lions (p.336), Alder Flies, Snake Flies and Scorpion Flies (p.340–41). Caddis Flies (p.318) also have two pairs of membranous wings but they differ from the others in being hairy and may look like moths. Bees, Wasps and Ants (p.88–127) often look as if they have only one pair of wings, even though they actually have two pairs. This is because the leading edge of the smaller hind wing is hooked on to the trailing edge of the fore wing.

Insects which have two pairs of scale-covered wings

Butterflies and Moths (p.18–87) are immediately distinguished from other insects by their large, often multicoloured, scale-covered wings. Caddis Flies (p.318) are rather similar to moths, but with hairy, rather than scale-covered, wings.

Insects which have only one pair of wings

In the Flies (p.128–79) only the fore wings are developed as wings. The hind wings are modified into small knobs which act as balancing organs – they can be seen quite clearly just behind the fore wings. Bees, Ants and Wasps (p.88–127) may be confused with flies for they often look as if they have only one pair of wings; however careful examination will reveal that they have two pairs of wings hooked together and they do not have balancing organs.

Making a positive identification

Once you have decided to which group your insect belongs, turn to the relevant section. At the beginning of the first seven sections, you will find a page which gives you detailed distinguishing features of the biological group together with illustrations of four representative species.

FIG. 1

Key to Size Symbols

Less than 5 mm

Up to 12 mm

12–25 mm

25–50 mm

50–75 mm

Over 75 mm

Following this there will be a spread for each major family, with other composite spreads where smaller families are featured. On spreads where major families are described you will find the name of the family at the top of the left-hand page, together with two other pieces of information: the number of species in the family and the length of the insect (wingspan is given instead of length in butterflies and moths). Size symbols also provide a quick guide to the insects' size (see Fig. 1 Left).

Four paragraphs of text will provide information which make positive identification possible. Throughout the text, numbers indicate the name(s) of the insects illustrated on the spread. The first paragraph, under **Adult Characteristics**, provides details of features or combinations of features characteristic of that family.

The second paragraph, under **Adult Biology**, gives you information about the biology of the adults, where they are likely to be found and what they feed on. If they bite, sting or cause skin irritation, a warning sign has been included in the illustration (see Fig. 2 Right).

The third paragraph, under **Larvae Characteristics and Biology**, provides a description of the larvae, whether they are pests, where they are likely to be found and what they feed on. A numbered illustration of the larva is included on many spreads.

The fourth paragraph, under **Common Species**, provides examples of common species in the family and gives details of the illustrations on the right-hand page. Names printed in **bold** are of insects illustrated in the book, those printed in ordinary type are not. English names are given wherever possible, but where insects do not have English names, their Latin names have been used instead.

Illustrations are of one or more common species from the family, and include distribution maps which provide at a glance information about the distribution of this family of insects in Britain and Europe (see Fig. 3 below).

FIG. 3

Distribution Map

- ● Members of this family are widespread or common in this area
- ○ Some species from this family are found in this area

Other Common Families

In many places throughout the book, you will find spreads of smaller or less common insect families, where up to four families are featured together on one spread. A brief description of each is given, together with some details of the biology of the animals.

Specimen Spread

FIG. 4

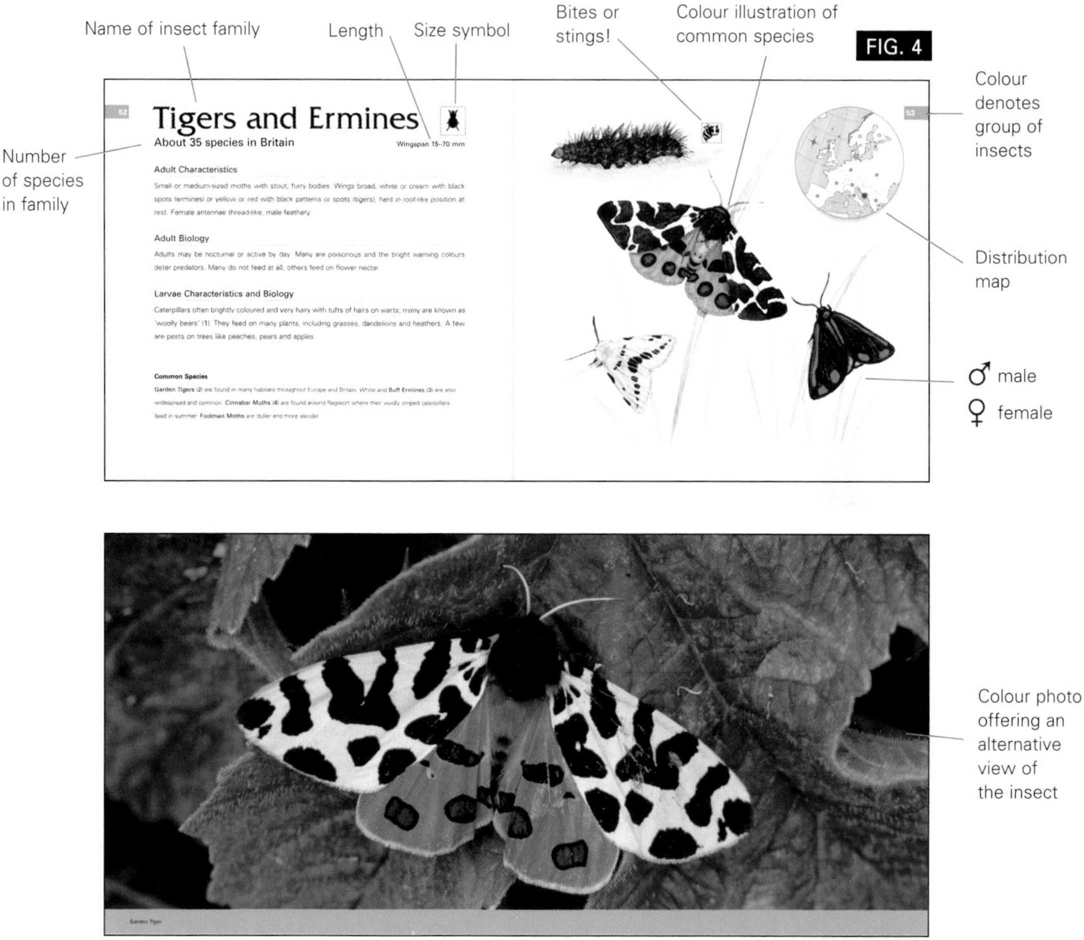

Name of insect family

Length

Size symbol

Bites or stings!

Colour illustration of common species

Colour denotes group of insects

Number of species in family

Distribution map

♂ male

♀ female

52

Tigers and Ermines

About 35 species in Britain

Wingspan 15–70 mm

Adult Characteristics

Small or medium-sized moths with stout, furry bodies. Wings broad, white or cream with black spots (ermines) or yellow or red with black patterns or spots (tigers), held in roof-like position at rest. Female antennae thread-like, male feathery.

Adult Biology

Adults may be nocturnal or active by day. Many are poisonous and the bright warning colours deter predators. Many do not feed at all, others feed on flower nectar.

Larvae Characteristics and Biology

Caterpillars often brightly coloured and very hairy with tufts of hairs on warts; many are known as 'woolly bears' (1). They feed on many plants, including grasses, dandelions and heathers. A few are pests on trees like peaches, pears and apples.

Common Species

Garden Tigers (2) are found in many habitats throughout Europe and Britain. White and **Buff Ermines** (3) are also widespread and common. **Cinnabar Moths** (4) are found around Ragwort where their vividly striped caterpillars feed in summer. **Footmen Moths** are duller and more slender.

53

Garden Tiger

Colour photo offering an alternative view of the insect

Life History of Insects

Basically, insects have two different kinds of life history. Primitive insects, including grasshoppers, bugs, mayflies and dragonflies lay eggs which hatch into nymphs, small wingless editions of the adults which often lead a similar life to the adults and which gradually develop wings as they grow and moult. The wings are fully formed and the insects are mature after the nymph undergoes the final moult.

By contrast more advanced insects, including bees, wasps, flies, butterflies, moths and beetles have a two-phase life cycle in which the larvae or young stages which develop from the eggs are quite different in appearance and habits to adults. After they have hatched, the larvae grow with each moult but never have wing buds. At the penultimate moult they change into a pupa or chrysalis in which dramatic changes take place, and the larva metamorphoses into an adult. At the final moult the pupa breaks open and the adult emerges. The adults mate and the females lay eggs, and the cycle of development begins again (see Fig. 5 Right).

Life Cycle of a Butterfly

FIG. 5

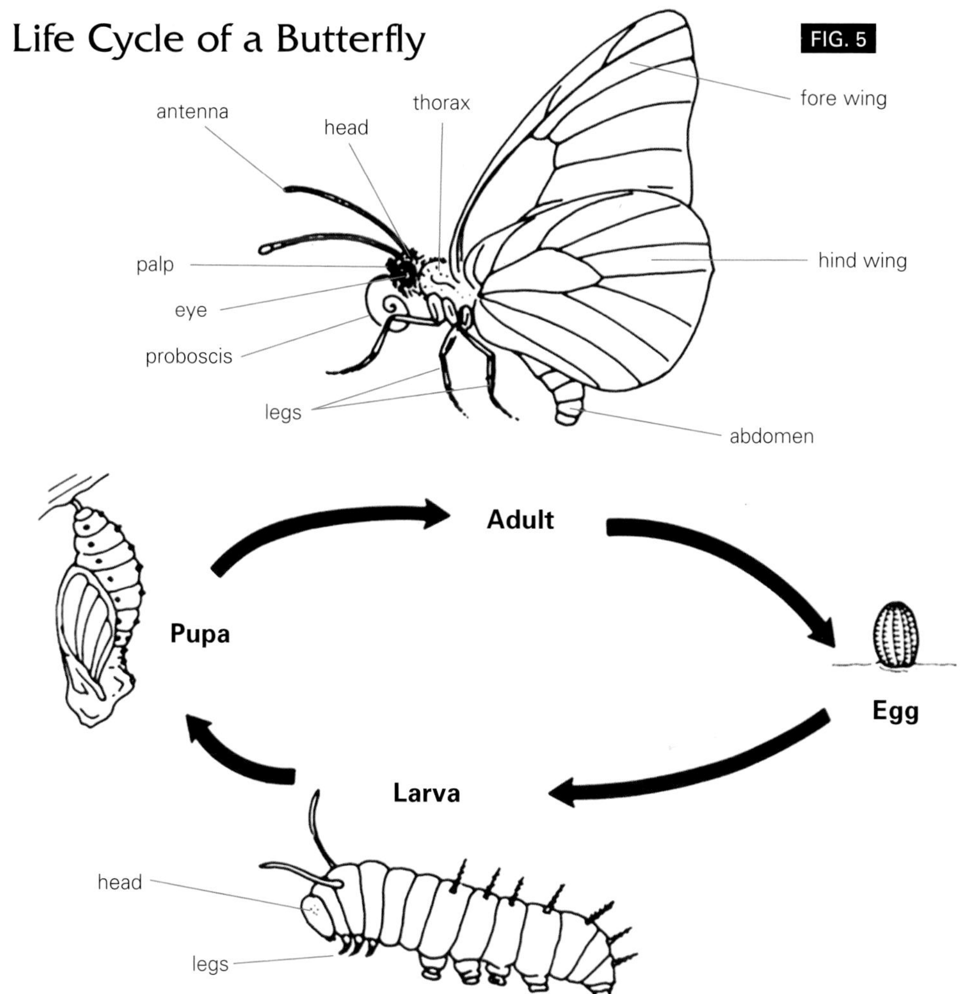

Illustrated Glossary

Honeydew A sugary liquid produced by some insects.

Moult Because of their hard skin (or exoskeleton), insects cannot grow continuously like many other animals; instead they moult periodically throughout their lives (shed their skin) and grow rapidly while the new skin is still soft, before the new skin hardens.

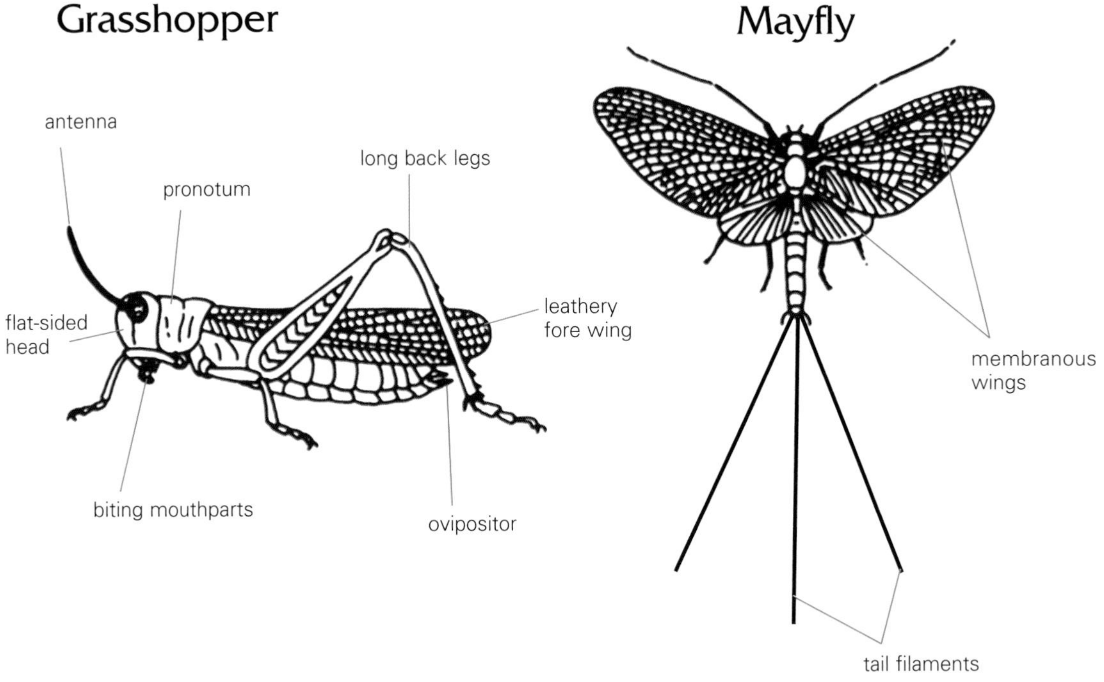

Bug

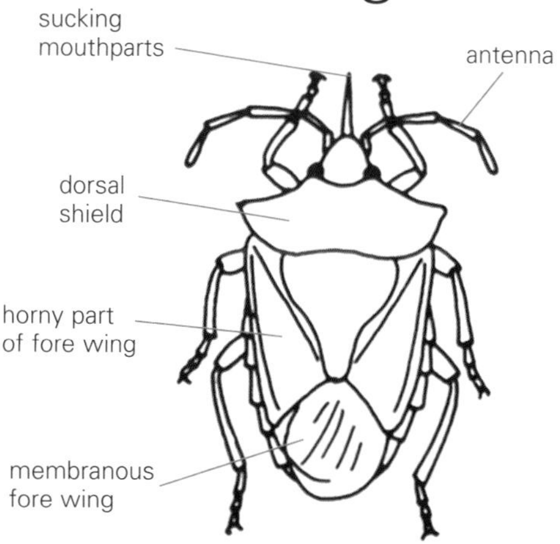

sucking mouthparts
antenna
dorsal shield
horny part of fore wing
membranous fore wing

Fly

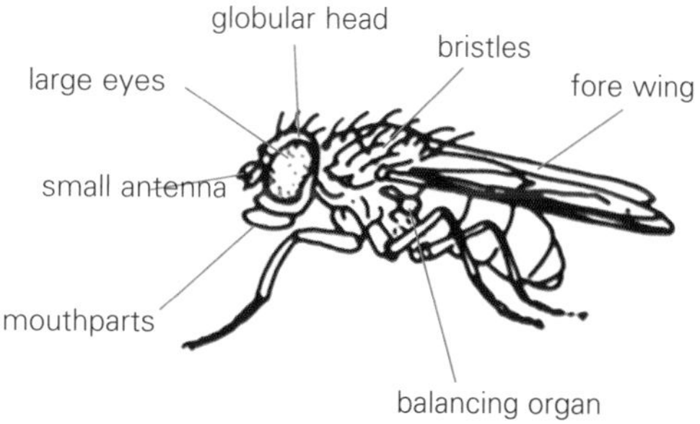

globular head
bristles
large eyes
fore wing
small antenna
mouthparts
balancing organ

Wasp

antenna
waist
joined wings
sting (ovipositor)

Beetle

antenna
pronotum
elytra

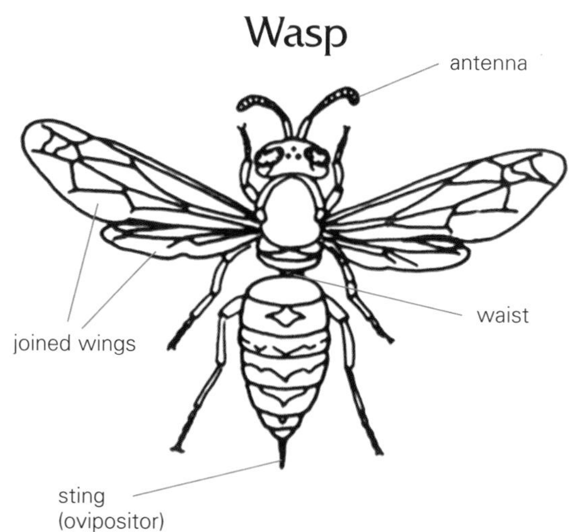

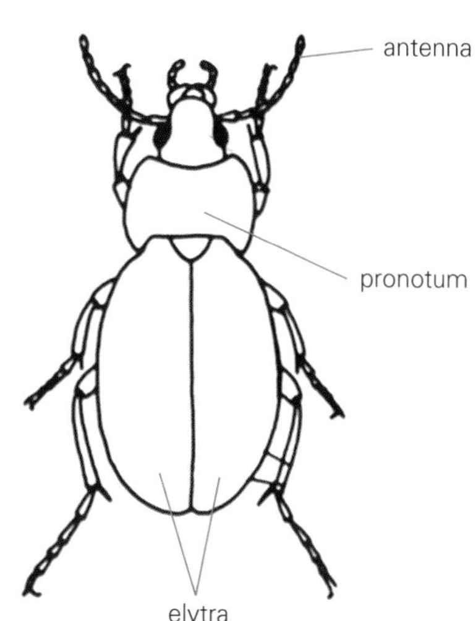

Butterflies and Moths

2300 species in Britain

Wingspan 7–150 mm

Adult Characteristics

These insects have two pairs of large, scale-covered wings, often with complex colour patterns. Scales come off easily. Antennae knobbed in butterflies, simple or feathery in moths. Many have a long proboscis coiled beneath the head.

Adult Biology

Most moths are nocturnal while butterflies fly by day. Many feed on nectar with their long proboscis which can reach far into flowers, others on sap or fermenting fruit.

Larvae Characteristics and Biology

Larvae are caterpillars; they have three pairs of legs on the thorax and usually five pairs of abdominal clasping prolegs. They feed by biting on roots, leaves or stems of plants and some do considerable damage. Many moths pupate in silken cocoons.

Common Species

Butterfly wings are vertical at rest; many have bright colours. Skippers spread their wings flat or raise fore wings and hold hind wings flat. Moths hold wings flat or in a roof-like posture; many are dull-coloured.

Marbled White (1); Green Hairstreak (2); Dingy Skipper (3); and Common Footman Moth (4).

1
3
4
2

Many butterflies have brightly coloured wings. Although this Marbled White does not it is nevertheless very striking.

Swallowtails

1 species in Britain

Wingspan 50–95 mm

Adult Characteristics

Large, brightly coloured, striped or spotted butterflies. Their hind wings are slightly concave on the inner margin and have a single anal vein. All three pairs of legs are fully developed.

Adult Biology

Most are found in rough ground in hills and mountain areas of Europe. Swallowtails have a powerful, gliding flight. Apollos and Festoons flutter and flap.

Larvae Characteristics and Biology

Caterpillars (**1**) usually smooth and mainly green, often with tubercles. They can protrude a pair of odorous 'horns' behind the head. They feed on various herbaceous plants.

Common Species

The **Swallowtail** (**2**) is the only member of the family found in Britain, where it flies in the Norfolk Broads. Several similar swallowtails occur in Continental Europe.

Also found in Europe are Apollos, white butterflies spotted with red and black, and Festoons with zig-zag patterns.

1
2

Swallowtails often have a pair of eyespots and 'tails' that can fool predators into thinking they are eyes and antennae.

Whites and Yellows

8–10 species in Britain

Wingspan 40–70 mm

Adult Characteristics

Small to medium-sized butterflies, white or yellow in colour, many with black markings. The hind wings have convex inner margins and two anal veins. The six legs are fully developed.

Adult Biology

Whites mostly fly with slow, fluttering flight, yellows more powerfully and rapidly. Mainly migrate through open countryside and gardens. Some live in mountain areas or rough hillsides.

Larvae Characteristics and Biology

Caterpillars (**1**) cylindrical, smooth in texture, green in colour often with longitudinal stripes. Caterpillars of many whites feed on plants of the cabbage family; those of many yellows feed on legumes. Some are pests. They do not make shelters.

Common Species

Large Whites (**2**) are familiar garden pests on cabbages. Orangetips are white with orange tips to their wings.

Brimstones (**3**) are found throughout Europe and Britain, appearing in spring and summer; however most Yellows, like the Clouded Yellows, are confined to Europe, sometimes migrating into southern Britain.

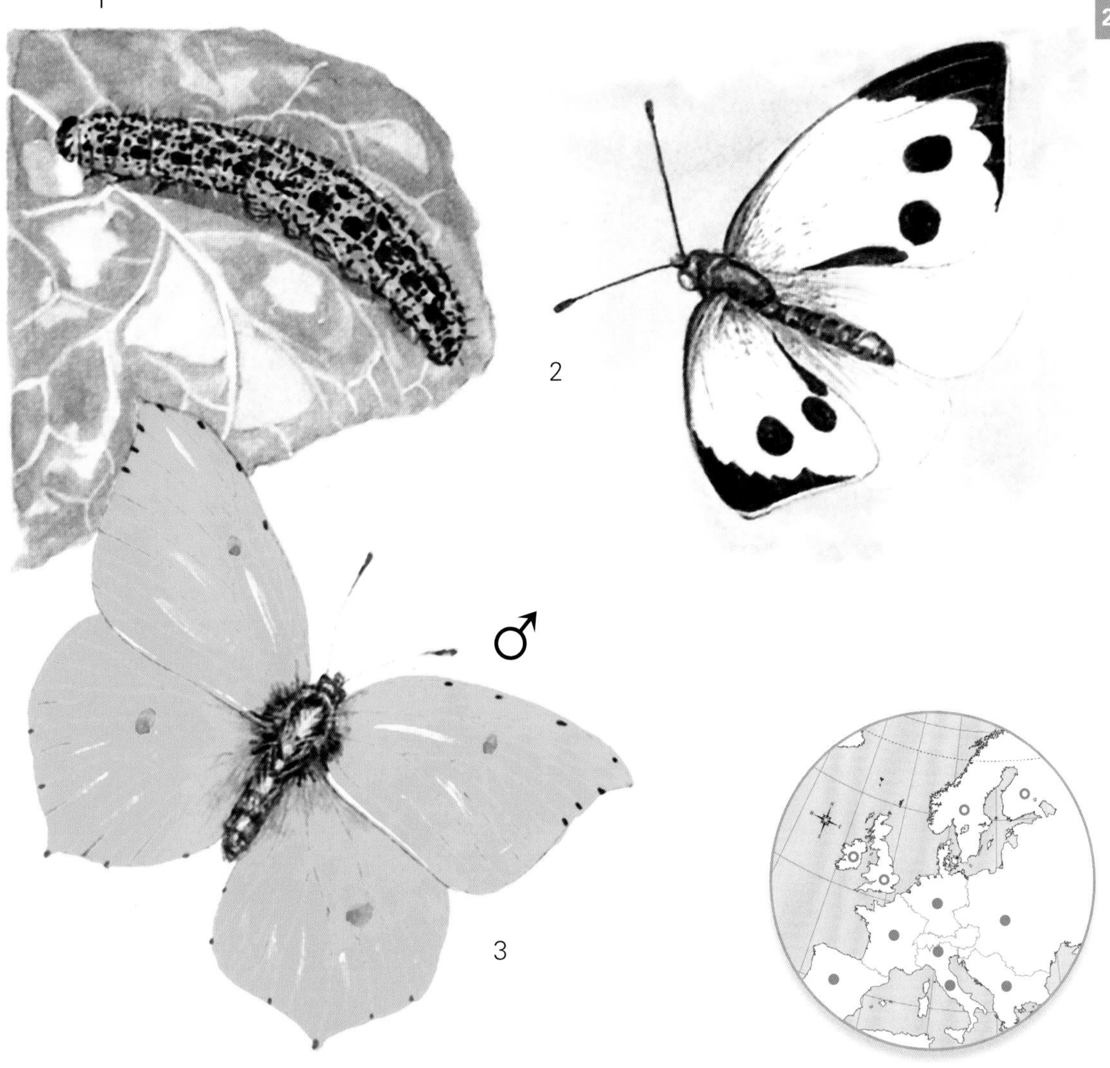
1
2
♂
3

The unique wing shape of the Brimstone acts as camouflage during hibernation and periods of rest.

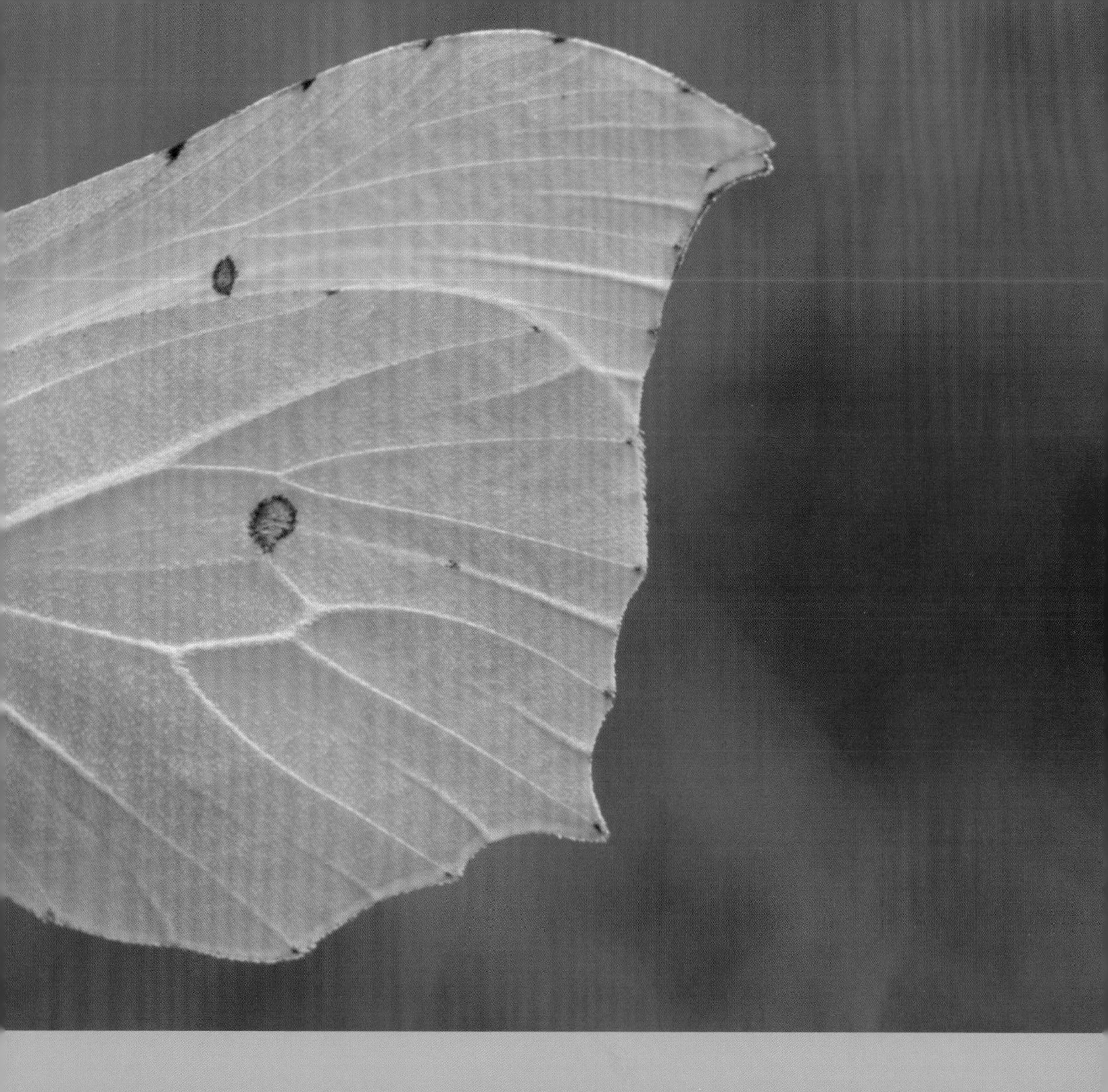

Blues, Coppers and Hairstreaks

Wingspan 20–40 mm

16 species in Britain

Adult Characteristics

Small blue, brown or copper-coloured butterflies, males and females often very different but both with similar spotted patterns on the undersides of their wings. All six legs are functional but males have claws missing on the forelegs.

Adult Biology

Blues and coppers are often found in grassy meadows, on grassy hillsides or in mountains. Adults fly rapidly, visiting flowers for nectar. Hairstreaks are mostly seen around trees or shrubs.

Larvae Characteristics and Biology

Caterpillars (**1**) flattened, slug-like, covered in fine hairs, tapering at each end. Many produce honeydew and are milked by ants. Caterpillars of blues feed on leguminous plants, of coppers on docks and sorrels, of hairstreaks on trees and shrubs.

Common Species

Male blues, like that of **Common Blue** (**2**) illustrated, are often bright, metallic blue; female blues (**3**) are brown with some blue markings. Coppers are orange-brown, like the **Small Copper** (**4**). **Hairstreaks** are usually brown or green, with blue or orange markings.

1
2
3
♀
♂
4

The Common Blue male can be a bright metallic colour, whereas the females are brown with some blue markings.

Brush-Footed Butterflies

Wingspan 35–80 mm

16–18 species in Britain

Adult Characteristics

Medium-sized to large, densely hairy butterflies, brightly coloured with complex patterns. Their fore legs are reduced to brush-like stumps in both sexes, hairier in the males; the other legs are used for walking. Antennae have very distinct clubs.

Adult Biology

Aristocrats are found in many habitats, several in gardens, fritillaries often in woods. Flight powerful but many stay in their territories and colonies; others migrate long distances.

Larvae Characteristics and Biology

Caterpillars (**1**) medium-sized to large, often with rows of spines on the body or horns on the head. Many live in communal webs, others hide in curled leaves. Some feed by night, others by day, on a wide variety of shrubs, trees and herbaceous plants.

Common Species

The largest of all butterfly families with many famous members. Peacocks, Admirals, Emperors, **Tortoiseshells**, **Commas** and Painted Ladies are often known as Aristocrats. Two of the most colourful are the **Peacock** (**2**) and the **Red Admiral** (**3**), found throughout much of Britain and Europe, except the far north.

2
1
3

The Peacock is part of the same family as the Red Admiral – both striking and well-known butterflies.

Brush-Footed Butterflies

Other members of the family include the **Comma** (**1**), with its angled wings, ragged wing margins and hind wing tails; and the European Map Butterfly with map-like marking on its wings. Tortoiseshells are colourful butterflies, red and brown with darker stripes and spots. **Small Tortoiseshells** (**2**) are found throughout Europe and Britain, Large Tortoiseshells mainly in the south and in southern Britain. The paler Painted Lady is a migrant species, migrating into Europe from Africa each year, reaching Scandinavia and Britain.

1

2

Brush-Footed Butterflies

3

The Fritillaries are a large group of butterflies, generally orange-brown in colour with complex black spots and marks on their wings, and often with silver spots or marks on the undersides. Many, like the **Silver-Washed Fritillary** (**3**), and the **Small Pearl-Bordered Fritillary** (**4**), are found in woods, where their caterpillars feed on violets. The adults are often seen around bramble patches, searching for nectar. Other species fly in mountain areas, heath land and flowery meadows.

4

The female Small Tortoiseshell lays her eggs on stinging nettles, which the caterpillar then feeds on when it emerges.

Browns

12 species in Britain

Wingspan 28–70 mm

Adult Characteristics

Mostly medium-sized butterflies, usually with wings in shades of brown or buff, often with spots or eyes, these sometimes set in a paler band. Antennae not strongly clubbed. Front legs of both sexes reduced to hairy brushes; other four legs used for walking.

Adult Biology

Found wherever there are grasses; usually in open meadows and marshes, on heaths, mountain slopes or arctic tundra, also in woods. Flight lazy and just above the vegetation.

Larvae Characteristics and Biology

Caterpillars (**1**) mostly green or brown, smooth in texture with longitudinal stripes and a forked 'tail'. They come out to feed at night, on grasses.

Common Species

A large family, most found in southern Europe and in the mountains. It includes Browns, like **Meadow Brown** (**2**), Satyrs, Graylings, Ringlets and Heaths, like the **Small Heath** (**3**); all have brown wings and eyespots typical of the family. **Marbled Whites** are atypical, with large patches of white on their wings.

1
2
3

The Meadow Brown is a member of the large family of Browns – all of which have brown wings with eyespots.

Skippers

8 species in Britain

Wingspan 25–35 mm

Adult Characteristics

Small black, brown or orange-brown butterflies, many with white markings. They have large hairy bodies and relatively short wings. Some rest with fore wings raised and hind wings flat, others with flat wings. Antennae thread-like, hooked tips.

Adult Biology

Most adults fly in sunshine with a direct, skipping flight. Many are found in meadows, rough grassland and grassy mountain slopes, hiding among vegetation. Males dart out at insects.

Larvae Characteristics and Biology

Caterpillars (**1**) are green and covered with many tiny hairs; they taper at each end, have a slightly constricted neck and a distinct head. They hide in shelters of silk-bound, rolled or folded leaves, emerging to feed on grasses and other plants.

Common Species

Chequered, Grizzled and Dingy Skippers rest with flat wings, Small Skippers with their fore wings raised. **Grizzled Skippers** (**2**) are greyish and white-spotted.**Dingy Skippers** are browner, also with white markings. **Small Skippers** (**3**) are plainer but brighter orange-brown. Others follow variations on these themes.

1
2
3

Kittens and Prominents

Wingspan 26–70 mm

About 25 species in Britain

Adult Characteristics

Stout moths with hairy bodies. Prominents have a tuft of hairs on the hind margins of the fore wings; these come together when the moths are resting and give them a humped appearance. Antennae feathery in many males, thread-like in females.

Adult Biology

Nocturnal and mostly dull in colour, camouflaged by day. Often found in woodland.

Larvae Characteristics and Biology

Caterpillars (**1**) usually feed on leaves of trees and shrubs. They vary in form but many adopt a threatening head-up posture when faced with a predator. Some are extraordinary, like the Puss-Moth caterpillar (**2**).

Common Species

Puss-Moths (**3**) and a variety of prominents are found around willows and poplars, camouflaged against the bark by day. Caterpillars of **Buff-Tips** (**4**) may defoliate willows, oaks or orchard trees. Pine Processionary Moth caterpillars move in single file, feeding on needles of pine trees; they can be pests.

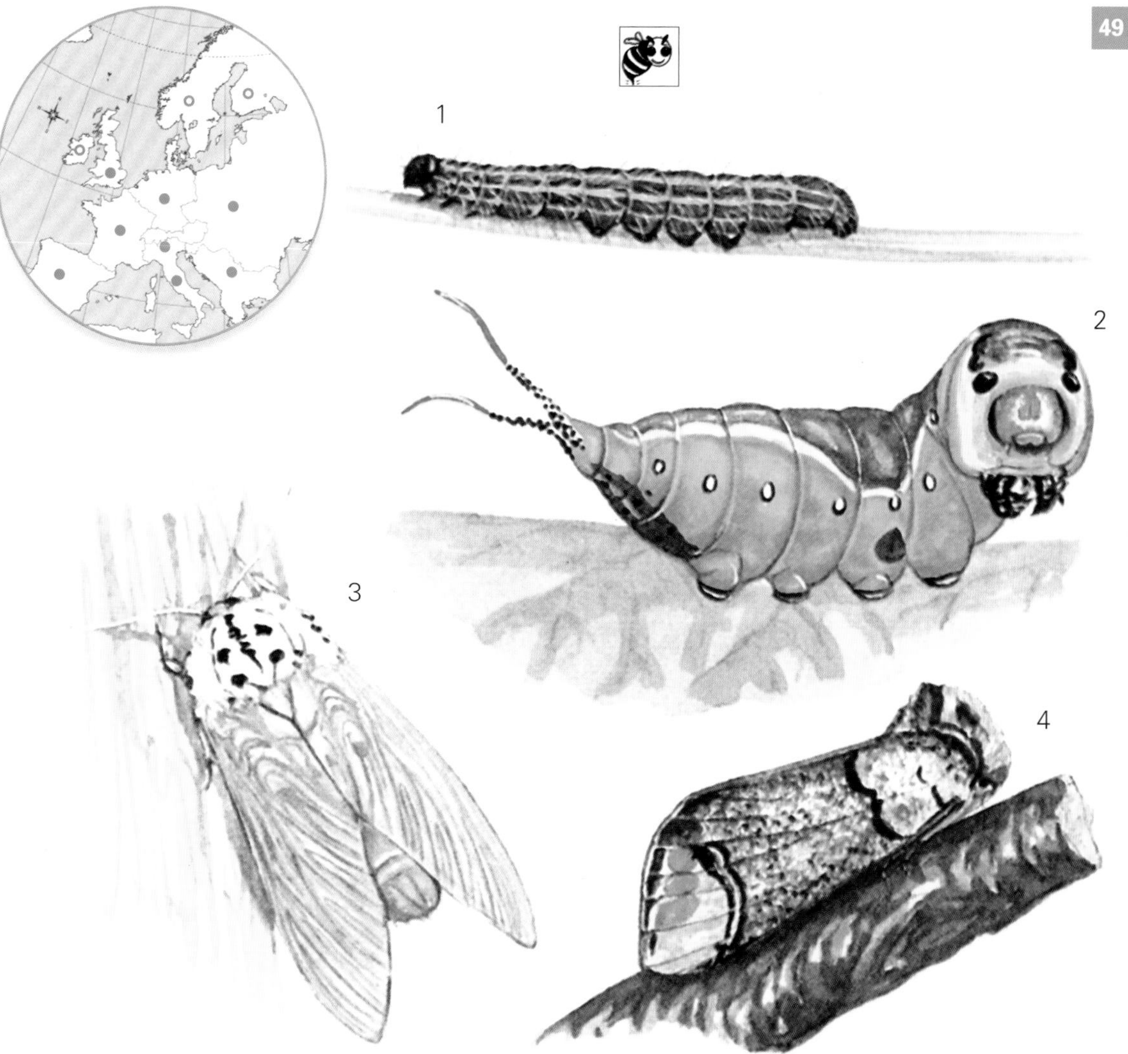
1
2
3
4

The Puss-Moth is one of a variety of prominents, which like to live around willows and poplars.

Tigers and Ermines

About 35 species in Britain

Wingspan 15–70 mm

Adult Characteristics

Small or medium-sized moths with stout, furry bodies. Wings broad, white or cream with black spots (ermines) or yellow or red with black patterns or spots (tigers); held in roof-like position at rest. Female antennae thread-like, male feathery.

Adult Biology

Adults may be nocturnal or active by day. Many are poisonous and the bright warning colours deter predators. Many do not feed at all, others feed on flower nectar.

Larvae Characteristics and Biology

Caterpillars often brightly coloured and very hairy with tufts of hairs on warts; many are known as 'woolly bears' (**1**).. They feed on many plants, including grasses, dandelions and heathers. A few are pests on trees like peaches, pears and apples.

Common Species

Garden Tigers (**2**) are found in many habitats throughout Europe and Britain. White and **Buff Ermines** (**3**) are also widespread and common. **Cinnabar Moths** (**4**) are found around Ragwort where their vividly striped caterpillars feed in summer. **Footmen Moths** are duller and more slender.

1
2
3
4

Tiger butterflies have stout, furry bodies, like the Garden Tiger shown, and their bright colours indicate that they are often poisonous.

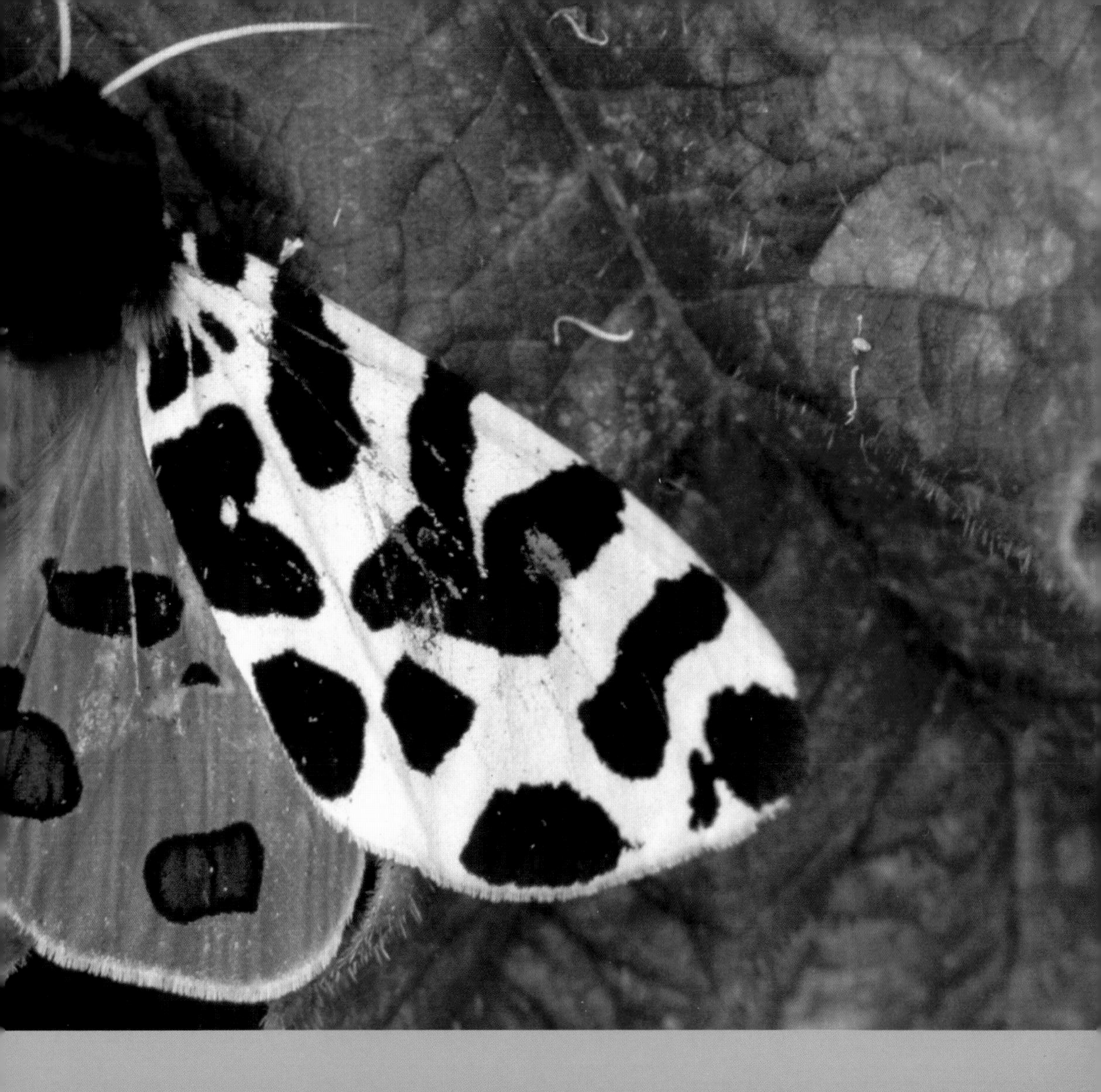

Noctuid Moths

Over 400 species in Britain

Wingspan 15–100 mm

Adult Characteristics

Small to medium-sized moths, with stout, clumsy, usually hairy bodies. Mostly dull grey, brown or yellow with complex patterns on wings; hind wings of some are brightly coloured. At rest wings look triangular, flat or roof-like. Antennae thread-like.

Adult Biology

Mostly nocturnal; often camouflaged to blend with background on which they rest by day. Many come to lights at night. They often feed on fruit juices or sap.

Larvae Characteristics and Biology

Caterpillars (**1**) dull in colour and hairless, usually striped or spotted; feed on leaves of wide variety of plants and trees. Some bore into stems and leaves, others (cutworms) hide in soil or litter on the ground by day, attacking plants at night.

Common Species

A very large family of moths. Some, like the Red or **Yellow Underwings** (**2**) have brightly coloured hind wings which flash as they take off, confusing predators. **Angleshades** (**3**) are a distinctive moth found in many habitats; it looks like a dead leaf when at rest.

1
2
3

The Yellow Underwings have bright hind wings which flash to deter and confuse predators on take-off.

Noctuid Moths

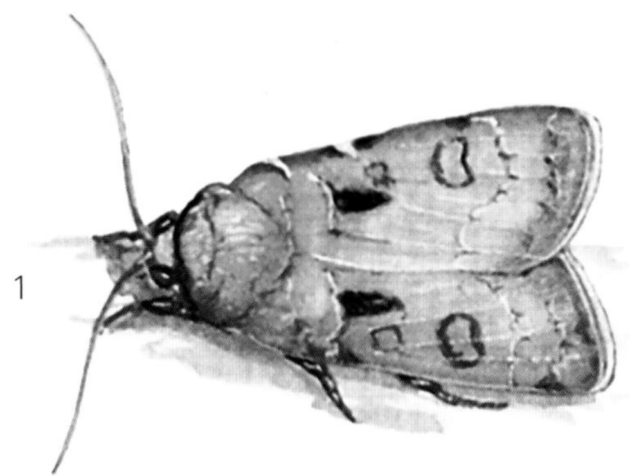

There are many moths in this family, given names like darts, daggers, sallows, wainscots, rustics, beauties, brocades, snouts and arches. In many species the caterpillars are cutworms, feeding on roots and stems of many different herbaceous plants; a few cause much damage in cultivated land and gardens, like the **Heart and Dart** (**1**). **Common Wainscots** (**2**) are common in damp grassland.

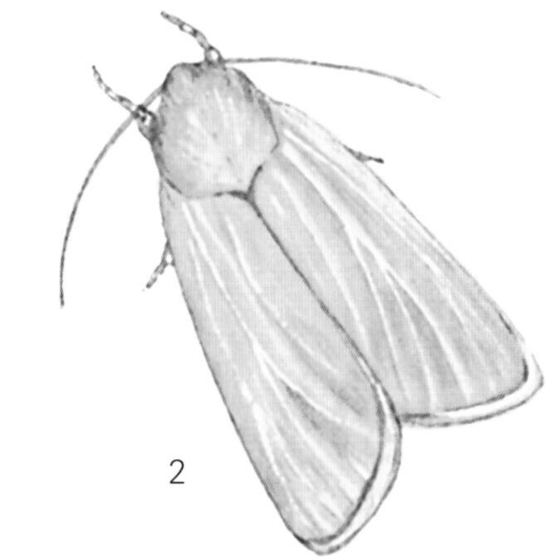

Noctuid Moths

Other species have caterpillars that feed on trees and shrubs, like the **Grey Dagger** (**3**); it flies in woods, hedgerows, parks and gardens and its caterpillars are found on apples, plums and hawthorns. Y moths have marks like the letter Y on their wings and tufts of hair on their backs. **Plain Golden Y** (**4**) lives in gardens and waste places where its caterpillars feed on nettles and other weedy plants. Peas and silverlines are greenish moths, with silver lines on their wings. Chestnuts are orange-brown, sallows golden yellow, brocades, arches, gothics and rustics all richly patterned.

3

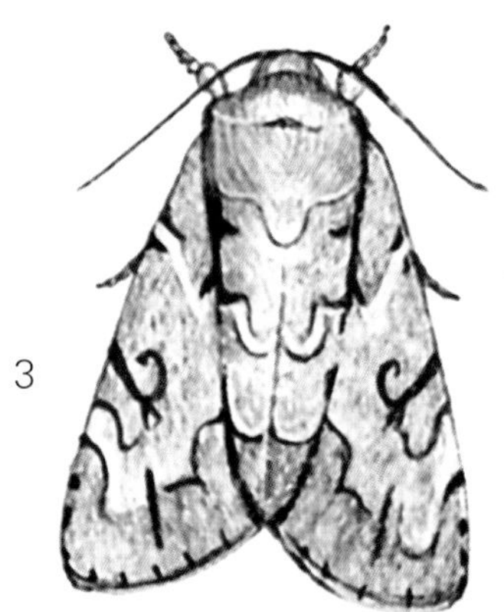

4

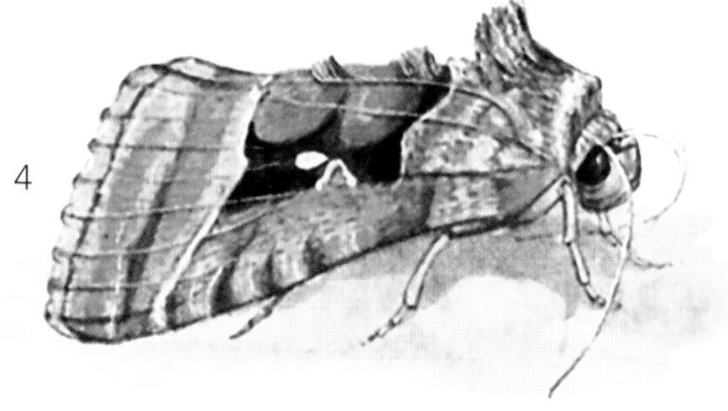

Geometer Moths

Over 300 species in Britain

Wingspan 15–65 mm

Adult Characteristics

Small or medium-sized moths, with slender bodies and broad delicate wings, spread out flat when at rest. Hind and fore wings are similar, often with patterns continuing from one to the other. Antennae feathery in males, thread-like in females.

Adult Biology

Many are nocturnal, grey or brown with cryptic patterns on the wings so that they remain camouflaged during the day, pressed against the bark of a tree or a lichen-covered rock.

Larvae Characteristics and Biology

Caterpillars (**1**) resemble twigs. They are called loopers from the way they move, extending the body and then drawing up the rear to form a loop. They only have two pairs of prolegs. They feed on many plants and may hang by silken threads from trees.

Common Species

A large family, with a variety of species. **Peppered Moths** have two forms; a speckled rural form (**2**) camouflaged against lichen-covered bark or rocks and a black city form, camouflaged against grimy trees (**3**). Many Emerald moths occur in Europe; the **Large Emerald** (**4**) lives in woods, hedgerows and marshes.

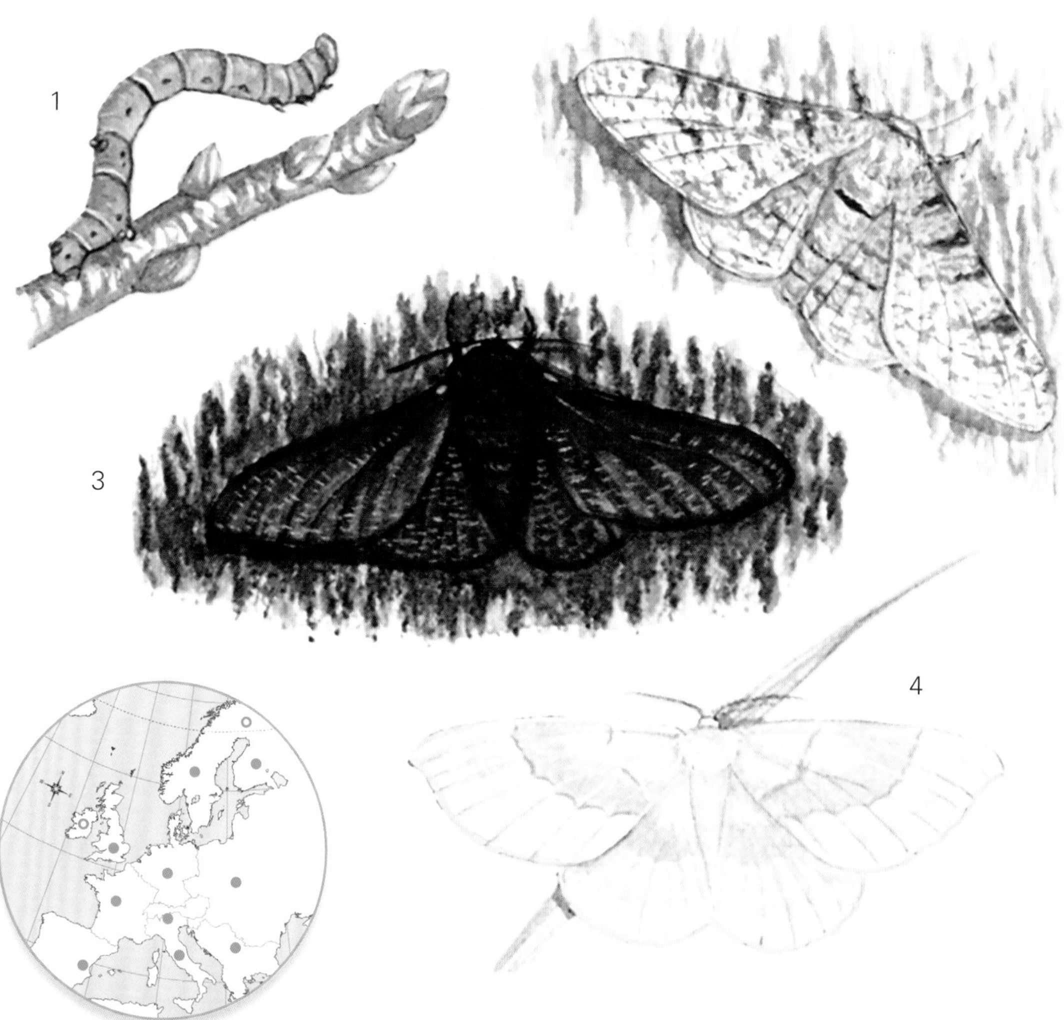
1
2
3
4

The Large Emerald moth lives in woods, hedgerows and marshes throughout Britain and the Continent.

Geometer Moths

Pugs, waves and carpets are small moths with wings patterned to provide camouflage. **Common Carpets** (**1**) are found in hedgerows and woods where their caterpillars feed on bedstraws. Beauties are larger moths; they also have elaborately patterned wings, in browns and greys that blend with the bark of many trees and shrubs. Their caterpillars feed on the leaves. **Winter Moths** (**2**) are pests on apple trees, the larvae feeding on young shoots and flowers; their females are almost wingless.

1

2

Geometer Moths

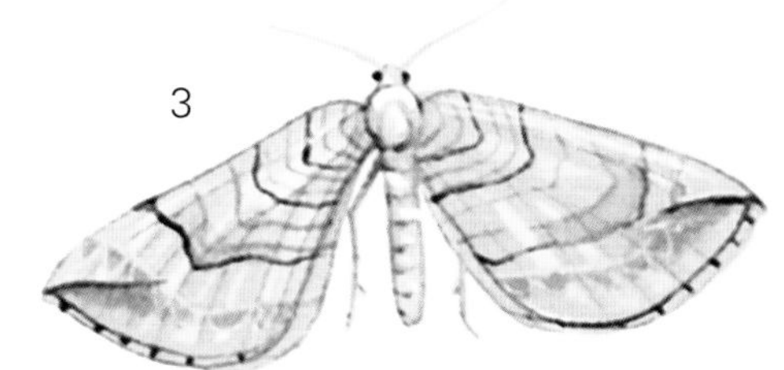
3

The Spinach (**3**) is another garden pest, the caterpillar feeding on red and black currants. Some species of the family are more spectacular. **Magpie Moths** (**4**) and their caterpillars are both spotted with black on white. They are found in hedgerows, waste places and gardens where the caterpillars feed on hawthorn and currants. Thorns have wings which resemble thorns when the moths are at rest. Caterpillars of **Lilac Thorns** (**5**) feed on lilacs, honeysuckles and privet.

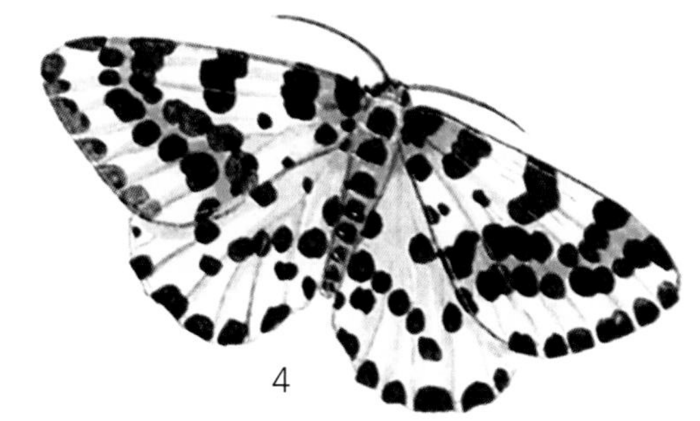
4

5

Like the Magpie Moth, its caterpillars are also white with black spots.

Hawkmoths

17 species in Britain

Wingspan 35–140 mm

Adult Characteristics

Medium-sized to large moths with heavy bodies and long, narrow, distinctively shaped, strong fore wings and small hind wings. Eyes large. Antennae thickened and spindle-shaped, with a bent tip which points upwards.

Adult Biology

Adults are strong, fast fliers and may migrate long distances. Most fly by night and may be attracted by lights. They visit flowers for nectar, sipping it with their very long proboscis.

Larvae Characteristics and Biology

Caterpillars (**1**) stout and hairless but often warty, with a large horn at the rear of the abdomen. Feed on a wide variety of plants and trees and some are pests.

Common Species

Elephant Hawkmoths (**2**) are found near willowherbs and sometimes near garden fuchsias (their caterpillar food plants). **Hummingbird Hawkmoths** (**3**) fly by day, hovering in front of flowers; they migrate northwards from southern Europe each year. Others include Death's-Head and Privet Hawks.

1
2
3

The Hummingbird Hawkmoth in action, using its long proboscis to sip nectar, which it feeds on during the day.

Other Moths

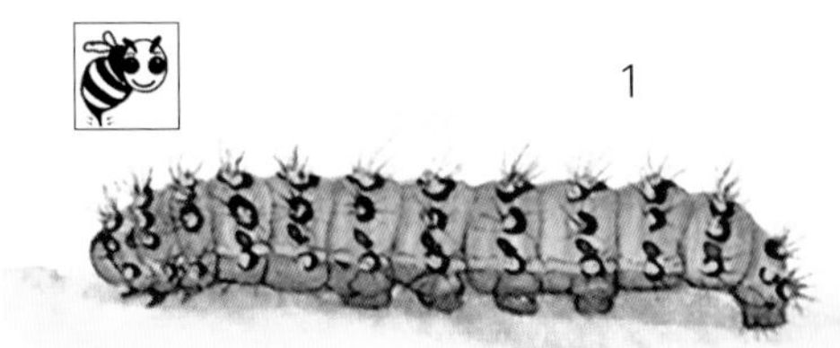

Emperor Moths

Large moths with stout hairy bodies, feathery antennae and huge, often brightly coloured wings with eyespots. Wingspan 40–150 mm. Proboscis reduced and moths do not feed. Caterpillars (**1**) large and fleshy, with tufts of hair often on raised warts. They pupate inside silk cocoons, like silkworms. Few members of this family occur in Europe and only one reaches Britain, the **Emperor Moth** (**2**), found on heaths and moors. The similar Giant Peacock is the largest moth in Europe. It is found in orchards and open countryside.

Other Moths

Eggar Moths

Eleven species in Britain. Medium-sized to large, hairy moths, with broad wings overlapping when at rest. Wingspan 25–85 mm. Antennae feathery. Caterpillars very hairy with irritant hairs. Caterpillars of **Lackey Moths** (**3**) live in colonies in silken tents on hawthorns, apples and other trees; they can be pests. **Oak Eggars** (**4**) are found in woods, on heaths and moors; their caterpillars feed on brambles, hawthorns and heathers. Lappet Moths resemble dried brown leaves when at rest.

3

4

There are just a few Common Emperor Moths in Europe, and only one of this heath-land species in Britain.

Other Moths

Tussock Moths

Ten species in Britain. Medium-sized hairy moths with barbed irritant hairs. Wingspan 25–65 mm. Proboscis reduced or absent and adults do not feed. Antennae feathery. Caterpillars hairy and irritant but attractive and brightly coloured, with tufts of hair on the back. Many feed on shrubs and trees; some are serious pests. **Vapourer Moths** (**1**) are found in woods, parks and gardens; females (**2**) are wingless, emerge from the cocoon only to lay their eggs on it.

Other Moths

3

Pale Tussock Moths (**3**) fly in woods and hop fields; their caterpillars can be pests. The larger Gypsy Moths are serious forest and orchard pests in Europe.

Hook-Tips

Six species in Britain. Small- to medium-sized moths, with narrow bodies, flimsy wings and hooked tips to the fore wings. Wingspan 20–40 mm. Caterpillars have only 4 pairs of prolegs (claspers are missing) and taper towards head and rear ends; they rest with both ends of body raised. **Pebble Hooktip** (**4**) is found on heaths and in woods.

4

Other Moths

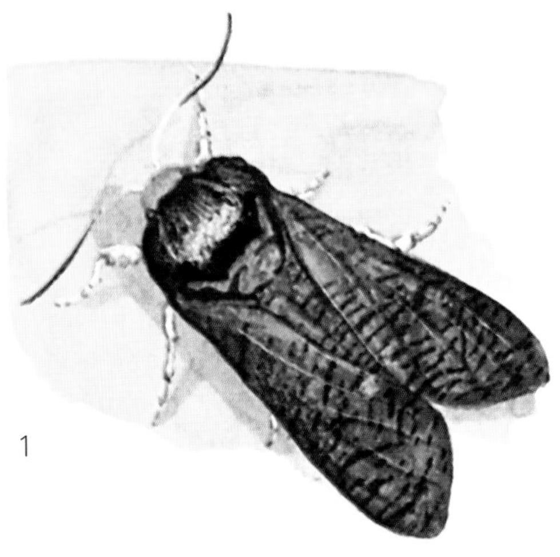

1

Goat Moths

Three species in Britain. Large moths (wingspan 25–85 mm). **Goat Moth** (**1**) is found in woods, gardens and orchards. Its caterpillars are large and fleshy and smell of goats; they bore into the wood of trees.

Burnets

Nine species in Britain. Day-flying moths with brightly coloured, metallic wings. Wingspan 24–40 mm. Antennae clubbed. Caterpillars stout with dark spots and tufts of hair. **Six-Spot Burnet** (**2**) is found in meadows, downs and woodland margins.

2

Other Moths

Swift Moths

Five species in Britain. Medium-sized moths (wingspan 24–62 mm) with very short antennae. Fast evening fliers, females larger and paler than males. Caterpillars live in soil. **Common Swift** (**3**) often comes to lighted windows.

Clearwing Moths

Fifteen species in Britain. Day-flying moths often seen at flowers. They have transparent areas on wings and often mimic wasps. Wingspan 24–45 mm. Caterpillars tunnel into trees. **Hornet Moth** (**4**) flies around woods and hedgerows.

Unusually burnets are species of moths that fly by day, moths tend to be nocturnal. The Six-Spot Burnet is found in meadows and woodland margins.

Micromoths

Snout Moths

Nearly 200 species in Britain. Small or medium-sized moths (wingspan 10–40 mm), often with large palps projecting forwards, like a snout. Fore wings are like long triangles, hind wings broad. Many are pests. **Meal Moths** (**1**) infest stored grain, with their caterpillars which live in silken tubes (**2**) and wriggle when disturbed. Caterpillars of China-mark moths live in water. **Small Magpie Moths** (**3**) live in waste places and hedgerows; caterpillars feed in rolled leaves of nettles, mints and deadnettles.

Micromoths

Leaf-Rolling Moths

Over 300 species in Britain. Small moths with fore wings shaped like a trapezium, broad at the base with straight, transverse borders. Wingspan 10–25 mm. Many fly by day. Most are mottled brown or grey, often camouflaged to resemble bird droppings or dead leaves. Caterpillars are often pests, infesting roses, pine trees, maples and other trees. Many live in rolled-up leaves, like those of **Green Oak Tortrix** (**4**), found on oaks. **Codling Moth** (**5**) caterpillars tunnel into apples. Pea Moth caterpillars eat peas in pea pods.

Micromoths

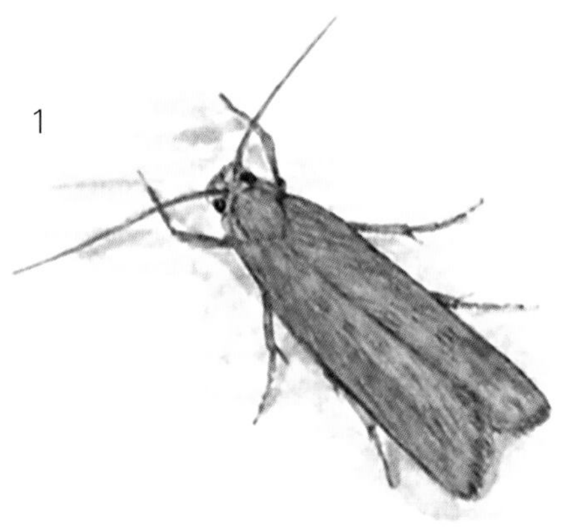

Small Ermine Moths (2)

About 50 species in Britain. Small to medium-sized moths (wingspan 24–45 mm) with white, black-spotted fore wings, grey hind wings. Caterpillars feed in silken tents among leaves of trees or shrubs.

Clothes Moths

About 50 species in Britain. Small brown or light-coloured moths (wingspan 10–30 mm) with a tuft of bristles on the head. Larvae of pest species, like **Common Clothes Moth** (**1**) feed on woollen clothes and carpets; many feed on plant and animal remains in the wild.

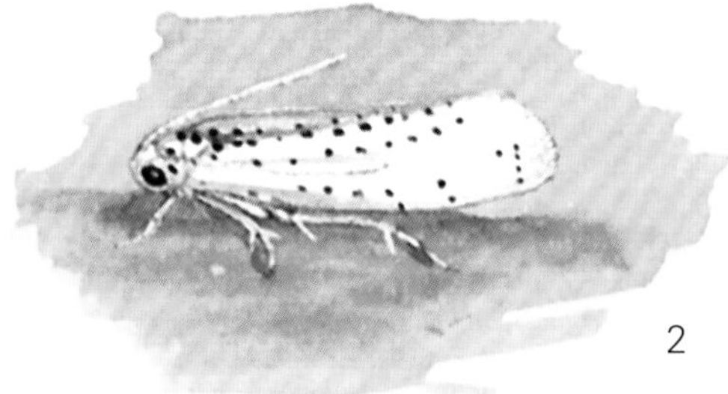

Micromoths

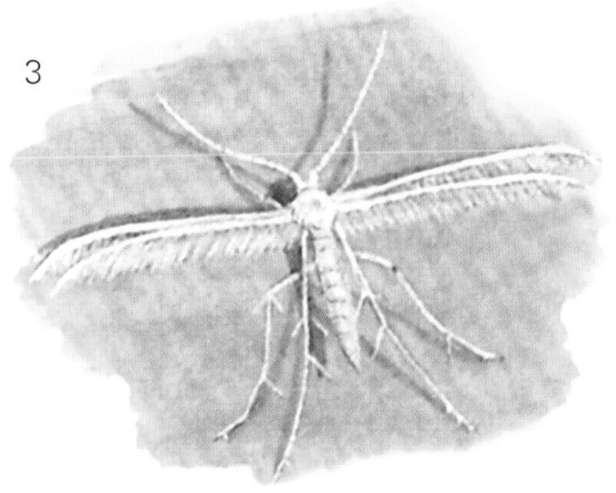
3

Longhorn Moths (4)

Ten species in Britain. Mostly day-flying, metallic moths. Wingspan 12–22 mm. Males may gather in swarms; they have very long antennae. Caterpillars are leaf miners when small, forming leaf cases as they grow.

Plume Moths

Nearly 40 species in Britain. Slender moths with narrow wings rolled and held at right angles to body when at rest. Wingspan 20–30 mm. Caterpillars are leaf rollers or bore into stems. **White Plume Moths** (**3**) fly in hedgerows and waste places.

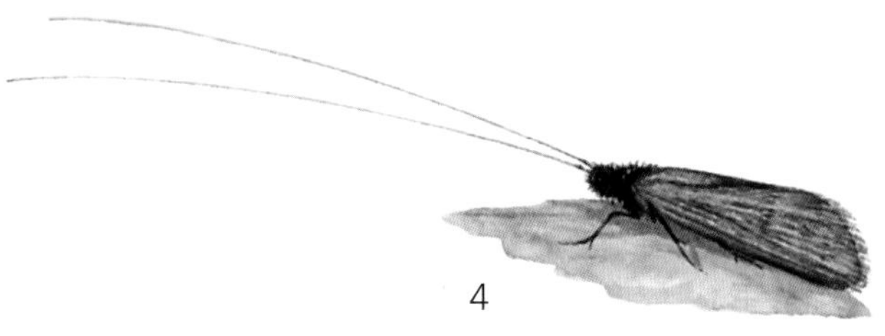
4

Bees, Wasps and Ants

Length: usually up to 30 mm

About 6500 species in Britain

Adult Characteristics

Tiny to large, often elongated insects, with two pairs of membranous wings, joined to look like one pair. Hooks at front of smaller hind wing engage into a groove on back of fore wing. Wings have few veins and large cells. Antennae quite long.

Adult Biology

Most are solitary but some are social, living in colonies. Many are essential pollinators of flowers. Parasitic species regulate insect numbers throughout the world.

Larvae Characteristics and Biology

Larvae parasitic on other insects, gall-makers or feed on plants. Sawfly larvae resemble caterpillars; they are often pests. Larvae of all others are white, grub-like without legs and rarely seen since they are concealed in host, gall or nest.

Common Species

Sawflies have no waist. Other species all have a distinct waist between thorax and abdomen: they include wasps, bees, ants and ichneumons. Illustrated here are **Horntail** or Wood Wasp, actually a sawfly (**1**); a **Velvet Ant**, actually a wasp (**2**); a **Flower Bee** (**3**); and a **Carpenter Bee** (**4**), found in Europe but not in Britain.

1
♀
3
♂
4
2

This Horntail is more commonly known as a Wood Wasp, but is actually a sawfly.

Sawflies

Nearly 500 species in Britain

Length: 5–40 mm

Adult Characteristics

Black or brown wasp-like insects, some with red or yellow markings; however they do not have a waist-like division between thorax and abdomen. Females have saw-like ovipositor. Antennae long and thread-like.

Adult Biology

Adults found around the larval food plants or visiting flowers, searching for nectar. Especially common on members of the carrot family.

Larvae Characteristics and Biology

Larvae (**1**) resemble caterpillars. On leaves they may do much damage, especially if they live in groups when they can reduce leaves to skeletons. Some are leaf rollers, others are leaf miners; some induce galls; others attack flowers or fruits.

Common Species

Sawflies attack many garden plants, including roses, turnips and newly formed apples. Larvae (**1**) of **Gooseberry Sawfly** (**2**) eat gooseberry leaves. Others attack trees, hawthorn, willows, larch etc. Larvae of **Pine Sawfly** (**3**) feed on young shoots. **Horntail** is one of the largest species; its larvae develop in pine wood.

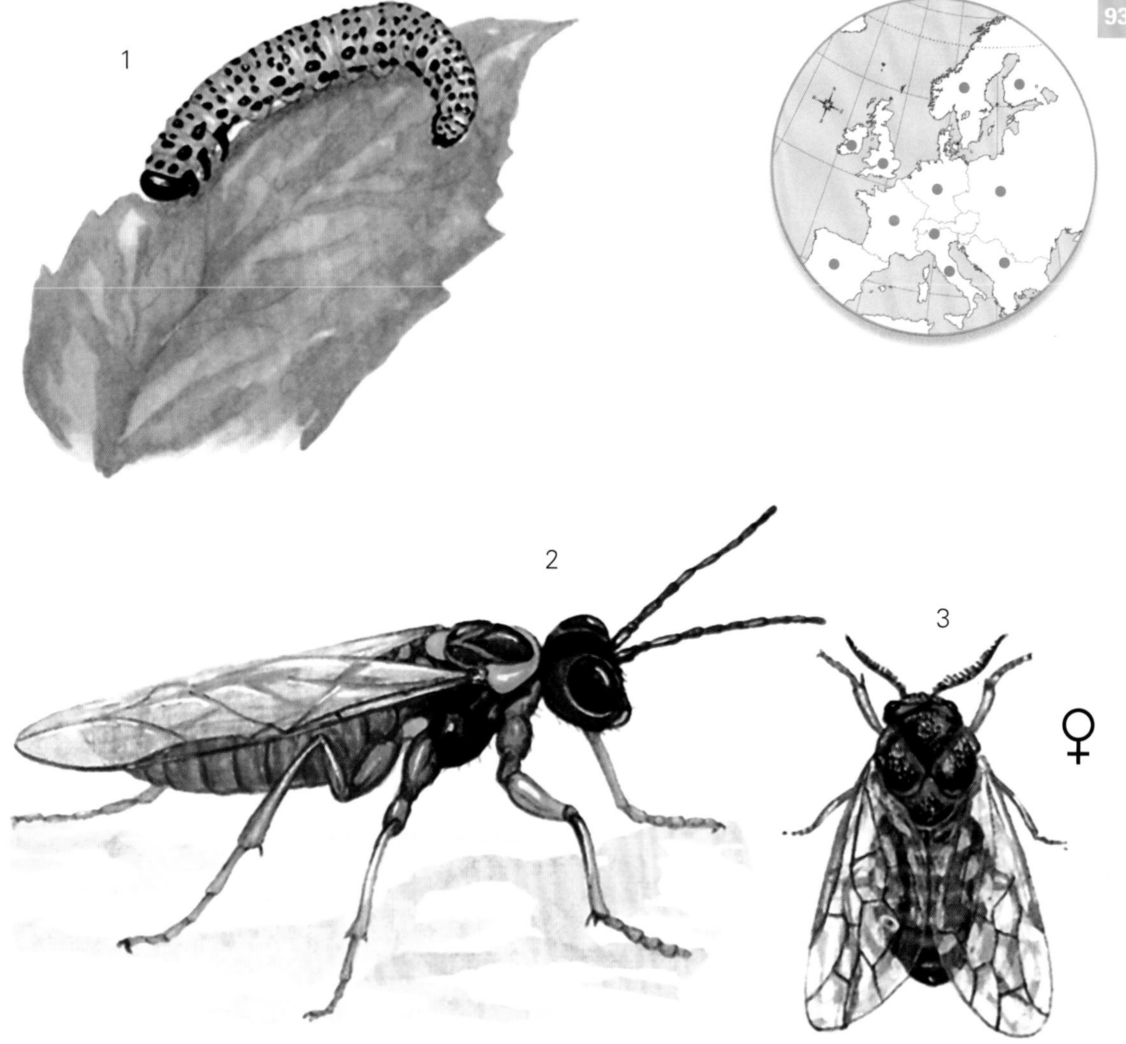
1
2
3
♀

Gall Wasps

Over 100 species in Britain

Length: less than 5 mm

Adult Characteristics

Very small, humpbacked wasps, usually black, brown or yellowish. They have a shiny, shortened abdomen, flattened from side to side. Antennae are long and not elbowed.

Adult Biology

Adults fly in spring and summer but are far less likely to be seen than the galls they induce on plants, mostly on oaks, but also on plants from rose, daisy and some other families.

Larvae Characteristics and Biology

Eggs laid on plants induce the formation of a swelling or gall and the larvae and pupae develop inside. One or many may be present. Some species lay their eggs on existing galls; their larvae develop as 'guests' and may destroy original inhabitants.

Common Species

Many gall wasps attack oak trees; their galls vary from circular spangle galls on leaves to spherical marble galls and **oak apples** (**1**); the latter are formed by ***Biorhiza pallida*** (**2**). **Robins' Pincushions** (**3**) are galls found on wild roses; they house many insects, not only the larvae of the gall wasp that induces them.

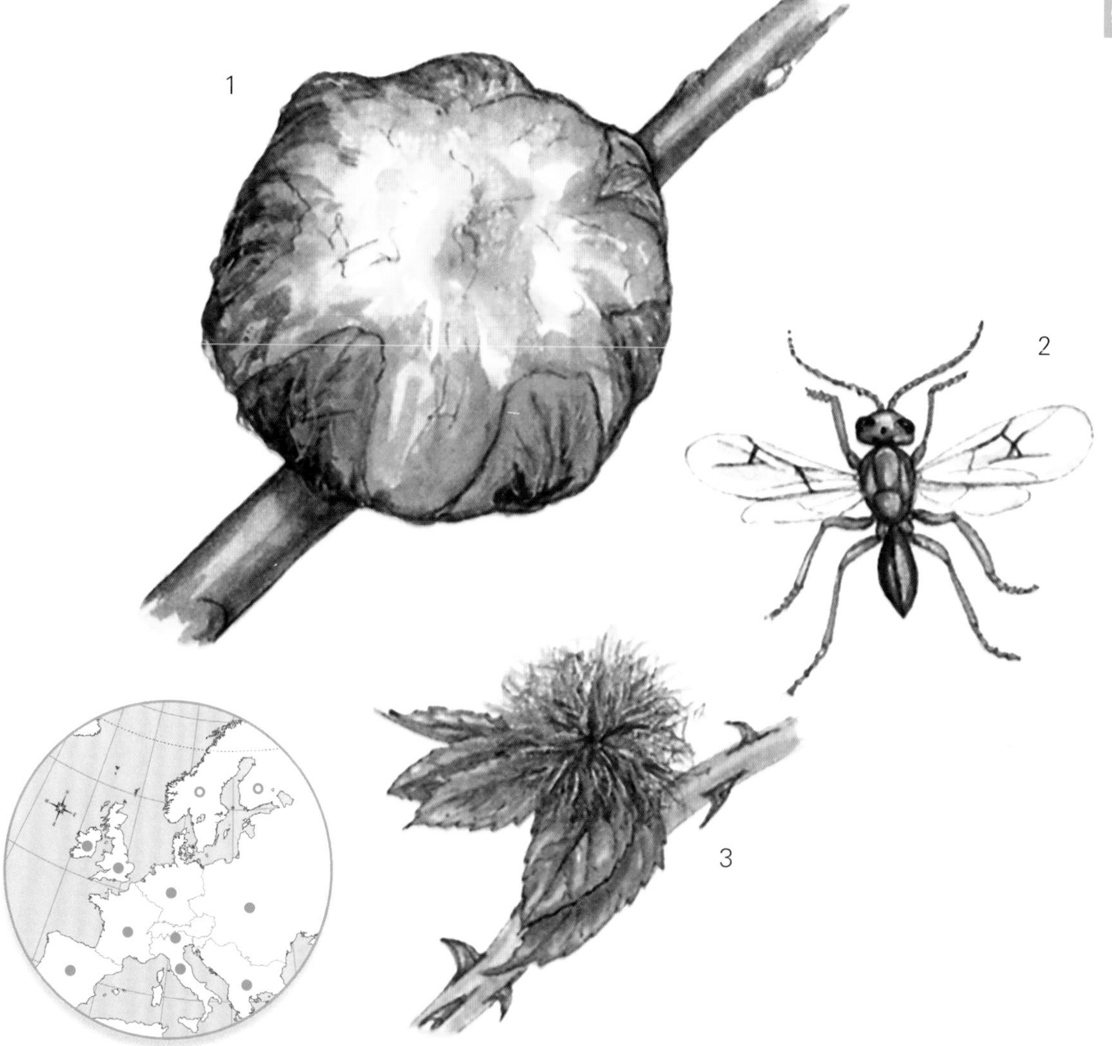
1
2
3

Chalcid Wasps

Over 1500 species in Britain

Length: usually less than 5 mm

Adult Characteristics

Very small, parasitic wasps with short, elbowed antennae. The veins on the wings are reduced to a single vein along the front of the fore wing. Black, dark blue or green in colour, many of them are metallic.

Adult Biology

Together with the parasitic flies, these wasps provide the most important controls on insect populations in the world. They occur wherever their hosts are present.

Larvae Characteristics and Biology

Larvae are mostly parasites on other insects. Females insert their eggs into eggs or larvae of a huge variety of insects, including flies, beetles, bees and moths and the parasitic larva develops inside the host, killing it.

Common Species

Most chalcids are parasites, like ***Pteromalus puparum*** (illustrated); its larvae develop inside pupae of white butterflies. Larvae of fairyflies, the smallest insects (some adults are less than 0.25 mm) develop inside eggs of other insects. Trichogramma flies are used to control greenhouse pests.

Digger Wasps

About 230 species in Britain

Length: up to 30 mm

Adult Characteristics

Quite large wasps with a slender waist between thorax and abdomen, usually black or brown with various markings. Their wings are held flat over the body when at rest. There is a characteristic 'collar' at the back of the head.

Adult Biology

Adults may be seen at flowers where they feed on nectar and catch small insects. They may also be found digging their burrows or hunting for prey for the larvae.

Larvae Characteristics and Biology

Solitary hunting wasps. Females of most species make a burrow in the ground, kill or paralyse their prey and leave it in the burrow with their eggs for their larvae to feed on. Prey include caterpillars, grasshoppers, flies and spiders.

Common Species

Very many of these wasps live in areas with sandy soil, where they can dig their burrows easily. In such areas **Sand Wasps** (**1**) can be seen dragging caterpillars and **Slender-Bodied Digger Wasps** (**2**) carrying flies to burrows. **Mournful Wasps** (**3**) are small black wasps that nest in posts, often in country gardens.

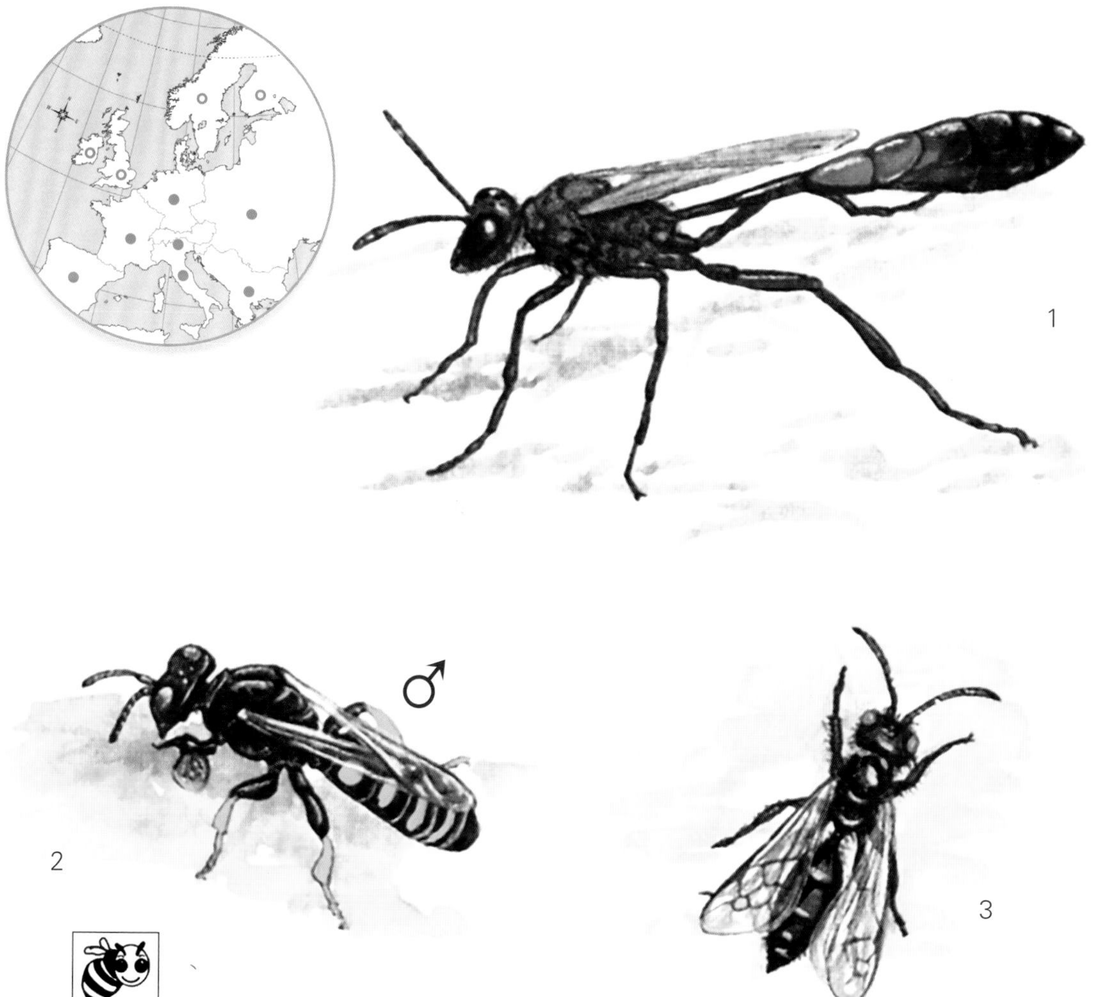
1
♂
2
3

Social Wasps

7 species in Britain

Length: 10–35 mm

Adult Characteristics

Black and yellow wasps with a distinct waist between thorax and abdomen. They fold their wings lengthwise when at rest. They have the ability to inflict a severe sting which can be repeated over and over again.

Adult Biology

Workers forage for food among flowers and rubbish bins; wasps may be pests in homes and at picnic sites when they are attracted to sweet foods and meat. In the wild they hunt other insects.

Larvae Characteristics and Biology

Social. Queens start nests in spring, at first with female workers only; males and young queens are produced later. Nests may be made in trees, in holes in the ground, in house lofts etc. They are papery in texture, with cells containing larvae.

Common Species

Common Wasps (1) are ubiquitous. **Hornets** (2) are much larger and rarer, and their nests usually built in hollow trees. Paper Wasps occur in Europe but not in Britain; their umbrella-shaped nests often hang from the eaves of buildings. Potter and Mason Wasps are similar but solitary wasps.

1
2

Hornets are much larger and rarer than the Common Wasp. Thier nests are usually built in hollow trees.

Other Wasps

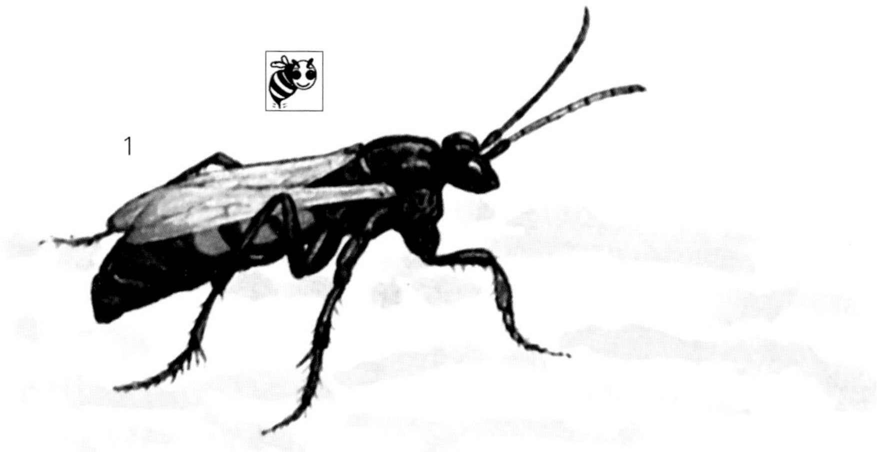

Spider Wasps

About 40 species in Britain. Long-legged black wasps, 5–25 mm long, often with red markings on the abdomen and dark wings held flat over back when at rest. Can inflict a painful sting. Usually seen at flowers or hunting on ground for spiders, often in heath land or sand dunes; they flick their wings as they run. Spiders are stung and paralyzed, dragged into burrow; an egg is laid on the spider and the larva feeds on it. **Black-Banded Spider Wasp** (**1**) is one of the larger species.

Other Wasps

Ruby-Tailed Wasps

Thirty-one species in Britain. Brilliant, metallic blue, green or red, hard-bodied wasps, up to 12 mm long. They do not sting but may curl into a ball if disturbed. Most often seen in sandy places, around walls and fences, looking for burrows of solitary wasps and bees. They are parasites with a cuckoo-like lifestyle. They lay eggs in burrows of these wasps and bees; their larvae kill the original larvae and feed on them and their stored prey. ***Chrysis ignita*** (**2**) mainly attacks mason bees.

There are 31 species of the strikingly coloured Ruby-Tailed Wasp in Britain, all with blue, green or red bodies.

Ichneumons

About 2000 species in Britain

Length: 5–35 mm

Adult Characteristics

Slender, wasp-like insects often with a very long abdomen. Female often has long ovipositor protruding from end of body. The black antennae may be marked with white or yellow and vibrate constantly; they are often as long as the body.

Adult Biology

Almost all are parasites on other insects; they are important in controlling insect numbers. Common in dense vegetation, hedgerows for instance, searching for insects among the plants.

Larvae Characteristics and Biology

Larvae are parasites, mostly developing in other insect's larvae and pupae, some in spiders. Hosts are mainly caterpillars, but also larvae of sawflies, wood-boring and leaf-mining beetles among others. Female can detect host in leaf or wood.

Common Species

Many ichneumons search for moth caterpillars to lay their eggs in; one such is ***Netelia testaceus*** (**1**). It is nocturnal and attracted to lights at night. The largest British ichneumon is ***Rhyssa persuasoria*** (**2**), found in pine woods; the females lay eggs in the larvae of horntails, through the bark of the pine trees.

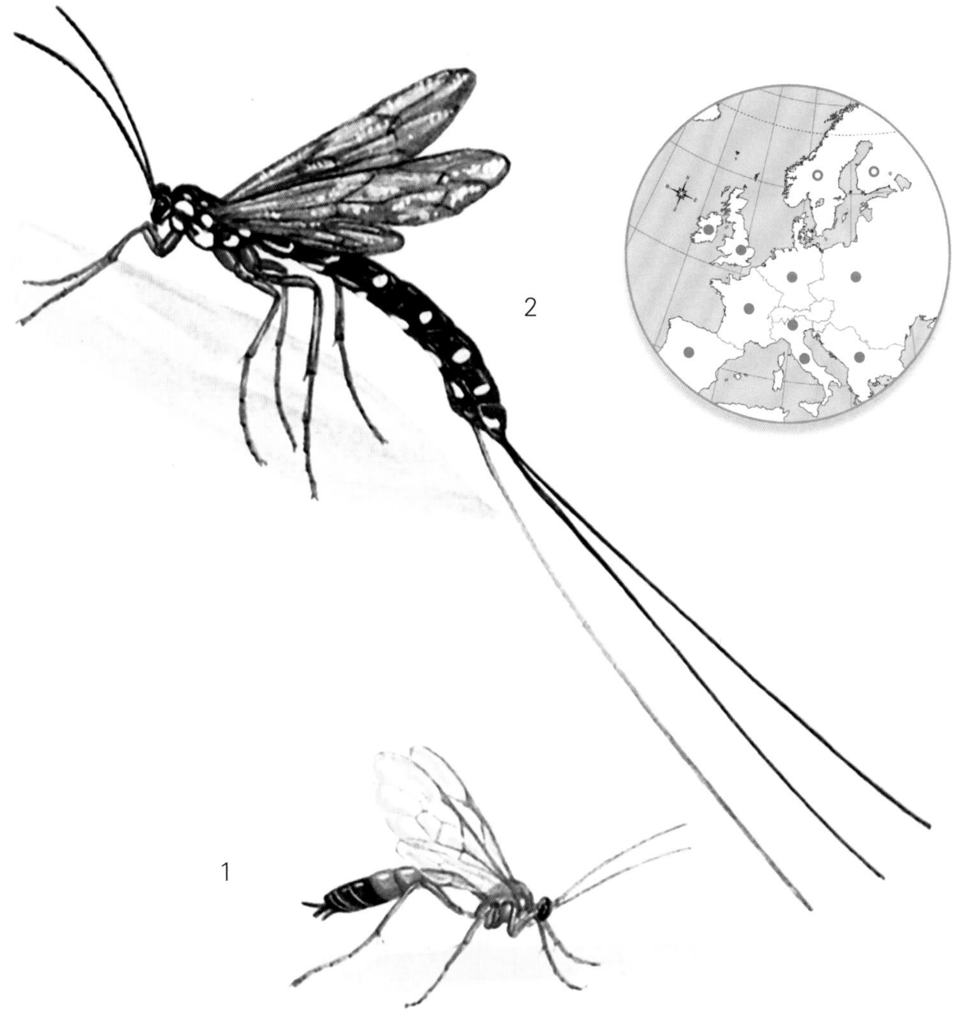
2
1

Ichneumons are parasites and lay their eggs in caterpillars. The female has a long ovipositor for this job.

Mining Bees

67 species in Britain

Length: 5–15 mm

Adult Characteristics

Mostly small bees, usually with black or brown abdomen and densely hairy head and thorax. There is a pollen brush present on each hind leg. They are short-tongued and so visit short-tubed and open flowers for the nectar and pollen.

Adult Biology

Among the first bees to emerge after winter. Pollinators for many plants, especially for spring flowers like willows and orchard trees, later for blackberries and the daisy family.

Larvae Characteristics and Biology

Mostly solitary. Females dig burrows in spring, leading to brood chambers; they may be numerous in sandy ground, in heathland, or on hard trodden paths. Entrance is tiny hole, at first surrounded by a small pile of earth.

Common Species

Yellow-Footed Mining Bee (**1**) is one of the largest of many similar species, but still only 12 mm long; its relatives are smaller and duller. **Early Mining Bee** (**2**) is one of the first to appear, around willows and dandelions. **Tawny Mining Bee** (**3**) nests in lawns, forming little mounds of earth.

1
2
♀
3

Mining Bees are tiny and often solitary. There are 67 species of Mining Bee in Britain, of which the Tawny Mining Bee, shown, is one.

Leaf-Cutting and Mason Bees

Length: 5–15 mm

35 species in Britain

Adult Characteristics

Small to medium-sized, dark-coloured, stout-bodied, hairy bees. They carry pollen on the hairy underside of the abdomen which often looks yellow as a consequence. They are long-tongued and have sharp, biting mouthparts.

Adult Biology

These important pollinators may be seen visiting a wide variety of flowers. Leaf-cutting bees cut segments from leaves or petals of many plants, including roses and willows.

Larvae Characteristics and Biology

Solitary bees. Females make simple nests of several cells, in holes in wood or in the ground; each cell contains one egg, pollen and nectar. Females then die. Larvae and pupae develop into males and females; these emerge the following year.

Common Species

Leaf-Cutting Bees (1) line and seal the cells of their nests with cut pieces of leaves. **Mason Bees (2)** use earth to build their nests. Some bees of this family are parasites on the others, laying their own eggs in the nests of others and removing the original eggs.

1
2

Bumble Bees

26 species in Britain

Length: 15–28 mm

Adult Characteristics

Mostly large, robust, hairy bees, usually black with yellow, sometimes red markings. Pollen collected in 'baskets' on broad hind legs to take back to hive. They have long tongues which can reach into long-tubed flowers. Will sting if provoked.

Adult Biology

Most likely to be seen around flowers collecting pollen for pollen baskets. Important pollinators of many plants that other insects cannot pollinate, including clovers.

Larvae Characteristics and Biology

Social. Only mated queens survive the winter, emerging in spring to start colonies, often in holes in the ground. Colony at first consists of queen and female workers who make nest of cells containing larvae; drones and new queens are produced later.

Common Species

Common species include **Buff-Tailed Bumble Bee** (**1**) and **Large Red-Tailed Bumble Bee** (**2**); both are frequent in gardens. Cuckoo Bees are very similar but have no pollen baskets on their legs; their queens parasitize other bumble bee nests, killing the rightful queens and laying their own eggs.

1
2

The Large Red-Tailed Bumble Bee is frequently found in gardens. They collect pollen in 'baskets' on their hind legs to take back.

Honey Bee

Length: 12 mm (workers); up to 18 mm (queen)

Adult Characteristics

Hairy brown bees with dark head and thorax, dull-orange bands on the abdomen and a black 'tail'. There is a pollen basket on each hind leg. The sting of these bees is barbed and they can sting only once and then die.

Adult Biology

Workers (illustrated) are pollinators for many trees, plants and crops. Seen around flowers collecting pollen. Many live in the wild, others in man-made hives. They produce honey and wax.

Larvae Characteristics and Biology

Social. Hive consists of queen and about 50,000 sterile workers, larvae and pupae, and males at some times of year. Swarm occurs when old queen leaves with many workers, to make a new nest. Young queen will rebuild old colony, after mating.

Common Species

Honey Bees all belong to one species, although there are several varieties. **Flower Bees** are larger, more like bumble bees, with furry black or brown thorax and striped abdomen; they fly faster than bumble bees and can hover. **Bumble Bees** are much larger with characteristic coloured markings.

The Honey Bee can use its barbed sting only once, and having done so it will die.

Ants

About 36 species in Britain

Length: usually up to 10 mm

Adult Characteristics

Generally small red, brown or black insects with first segments of abdomen narrowed into nodular waist. Antennae elbowed. Fertile males and females are winged forms which swarm; workers are wingless. Most bite if disturbed, some spray acid.

Adult Biology

Ants are often scavengers and some become pests in homes and picnic sites where they are attracted to sugary foods. Some tend and defend aphids, and milk them for their honeydew.

Larvae Characteristics and Biology

Social. Nest made in soil, in piles of sticks and pine needles, or in rotten wood. Consists of queen and workers; some species also have soldiers. At certain times of year winged males and larger winged females swarm; females start new nests.

Common Species

Black Garden Ants (1) are common in gardens and in the wild; they do not bite. **Red Ants (2)** nest under tree trunks or walls; they are aggressive and have painful bites. Wood Ants are large brown ants which bite and spray acid if disturbed; they build mounded nests in woods and heaths, of twigs, pine needles, etc.

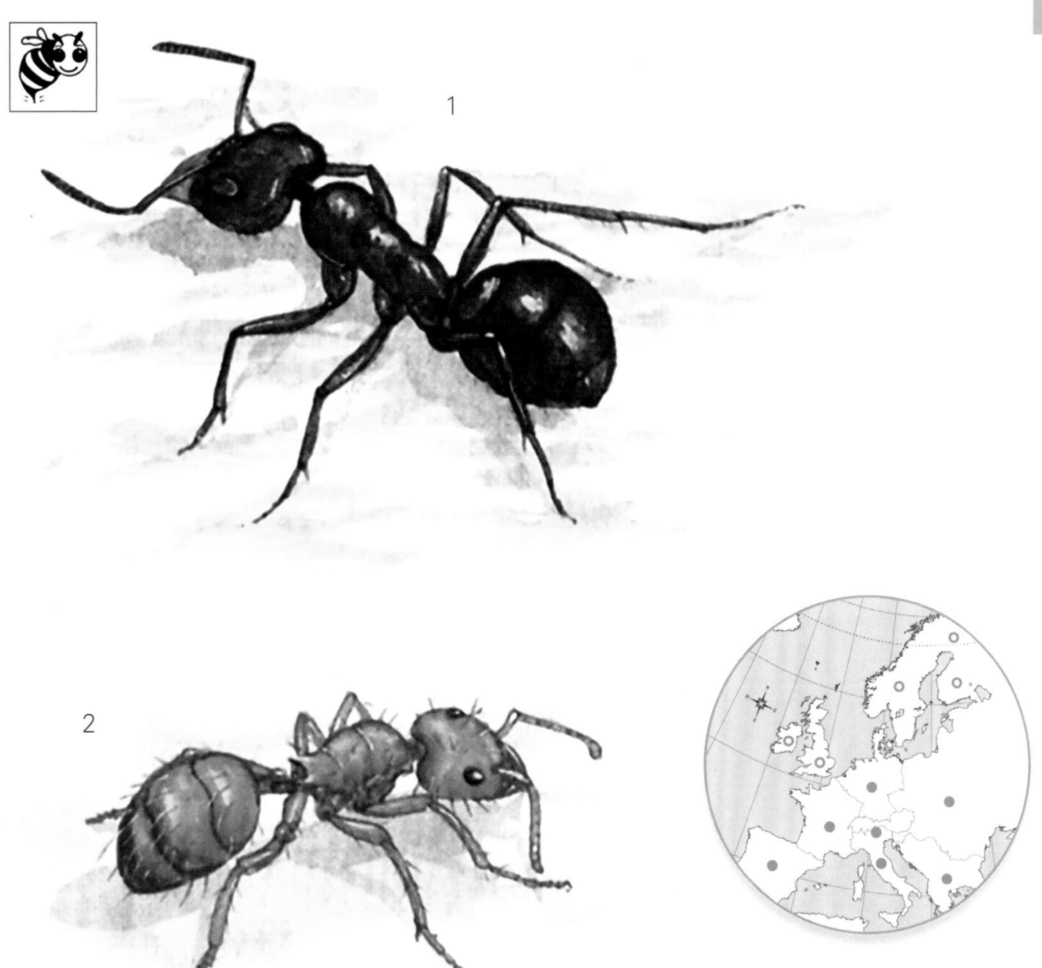
1
2

Flies

About 5200 species in Britain

Length: up to 32 mm

Adult Characteristics

Soft-bodied or leathery insects, often covered with bristles. Head globular with large eyes. Thorax oval and hump-backed. One pair of wings, the membranous fore wings. Hind wings modified as knob-like balancing organs.

Adult Biology

Adults found in many habitats, often around flowers searching for nectar; or near places where they lay their eggs, such as dung or carrion; or around larval hosts if they are parasites.

Larvae Characteristics and Biology

Larvae are soft legless grubs or 'maggots', many without well-defined heads. They adopt a variety of lifestyles. They may live in ponds, streams or soil; induce galls on plants; be parasites on other animals; or live in dung or carrion.

Common Species

There are three major groups of flies. Primitive flies (e.g. crane flies) have long antennae; in the second group the antennae are short but segmented (e.g. horse flies); and in the third, antennae are only bristles (e.g. house flies). **Winter Gnat** (1); **Carrot Fly** (2); **Large-Headed Fly** (3); and **Flesh Fly** (4) are illustrated.

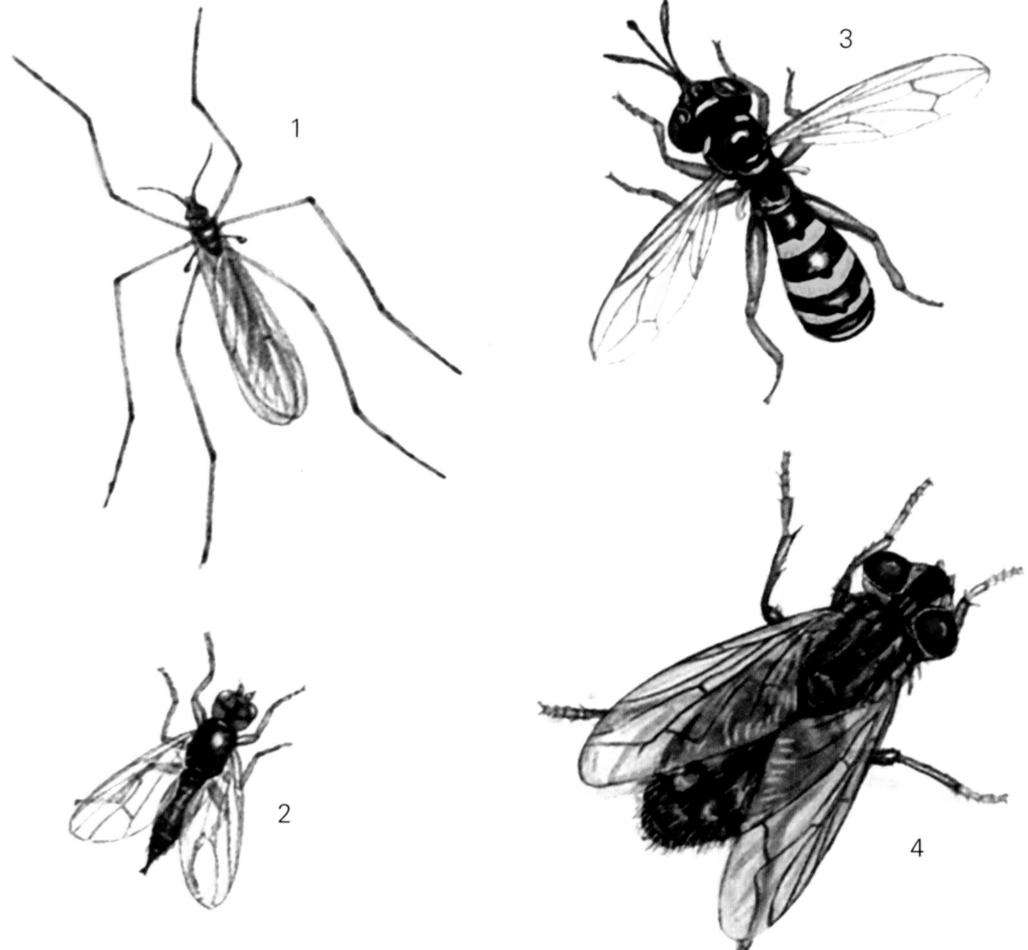
1
2
3
4

Mosquitoes

About 30 species in Britain

Length: 5–10 mm

Adult Characteristics

Slender, long-legged flies with a long, piercing proboscis with which females suck blood of people, mammals or birds. Males feed on nectar. Long antennae are feathery in male, hair-like in female. Hind legs are raised when they land.

Adult Biology

Found in damp places, woods, gardens etc. Most active at dusk and dawn. Females require a meal of blood before laying eggs. Birds and dragonflies hunt and feed on mosquitoes.

Larvae Characteristics and Biology

Larvae (**1**) are found in almost any small pond or puddle, ditches, streams etc. They may be seen, together with the pupae (**2**), hanging beneath the water film when they come up for air. They feed on plankton.

Common Species

Some ***Anopheles*** species transmit diseases (e.g. Malaria). ***Culiseta annulata*** (**3**) is a large mosquito, found in many habitats, often in houses; it bites people, causing inflammation. Common Gnats rarely bite people, preferring birds. Phantom midges (with feathery antennae) lack the proboscis and do not bite.

♀

2
1

The female Mosquitoes feed by sucking blood from mammals and birds. The males, however, feed on nectar.

Midges

About 380 species in Britain

Length: up to 12 mm

Adult Characteristics

Fragile, slender flies with poorly developed mouthparts and no piercing proboscis. Humped thorax conceals the head from above. Alight with fore legs raised, rest with wings held roof-wise over body. Antennae of male feathery, of female hair-like.

Adult Biology

Many adult midges do not feed at all. Males often appear in large swarms in winter or early spring, mostly in the afternoon near sunset. Females rest on vegetation near the swarm.

Larvae Characteristics and Biology

Some larvae live in decaying vegetation but many are aquatic, living in streams, rivers and ponds, often making a tube in mud at the bottom. They are soft-bodied and worm-like, some are bright red bloodworms (**1**). They are important food for fishes.

Common Species

Chironomus plumosus (**2**) is one of many similar species, whose larvae are bloodworms. Males may be confused with phantom midges. **Biting Midges** are similar but minute (5 mm long at most) and their wings are folded flat when they rest. **Mosquitoes** have a long, piercing proboscis and hind legs raised at rest.

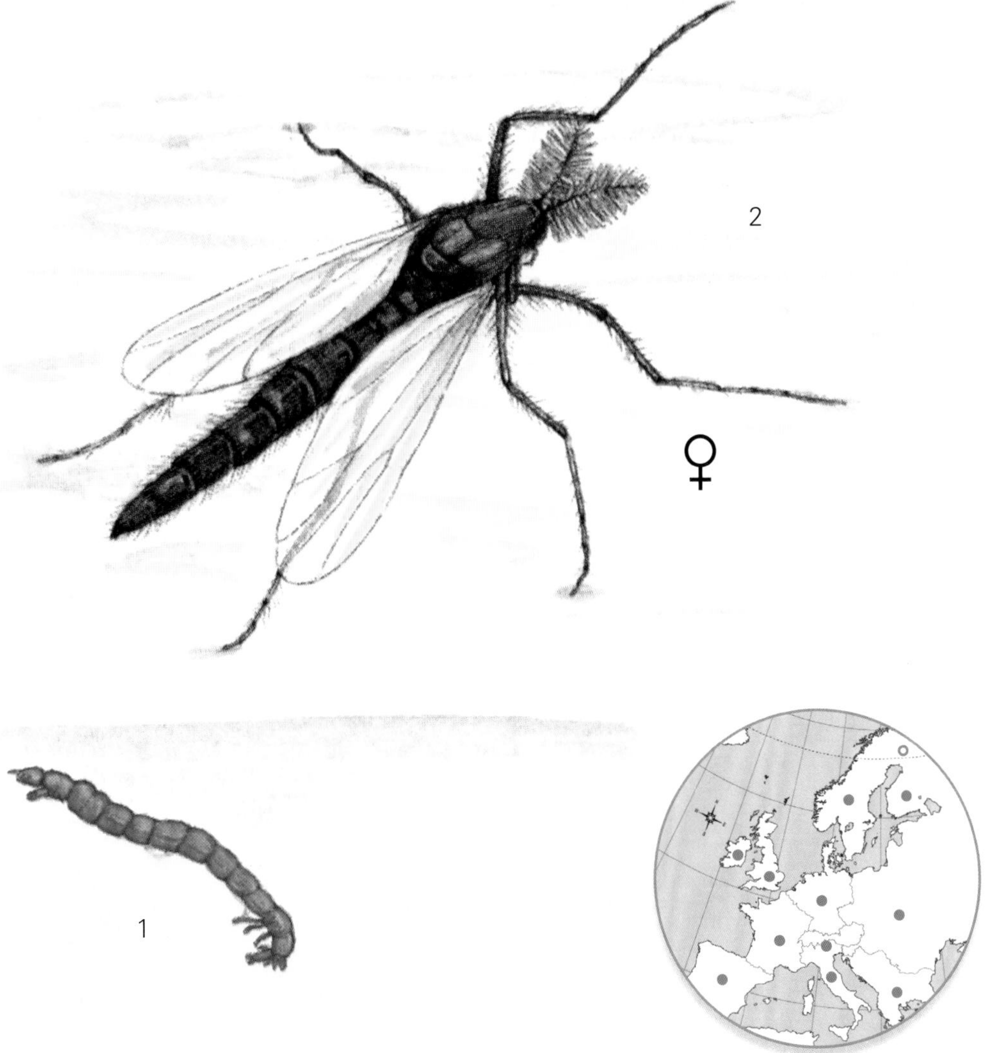
2
♀
1

Other Midges

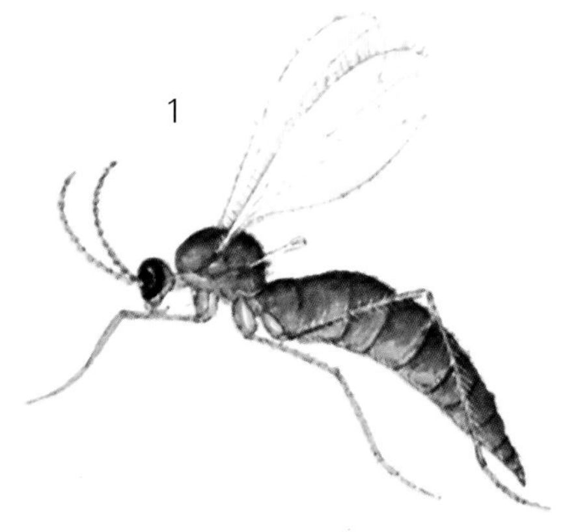

Gall Midges

Over 600 species in Britain. Tiny slender flies, up to 5 mm long, with long legs and broad, often fringed, hairy wings. Antennae bead-like, with whorls of tiny hairs. Flies less likely to be seen than the effects of their larvae on plants: distorted fruits, flowers and buds; tumour-like galls on stems, leaves or twigs. Larvae of **Hessian Flies** (**1**) attack cereals in southern Europe, boring into stems. **Chrysanthemum Gall Midges** (**2**) cause cone-shaped galls on chrysanthemums (**3**), distorting badly affected plants.

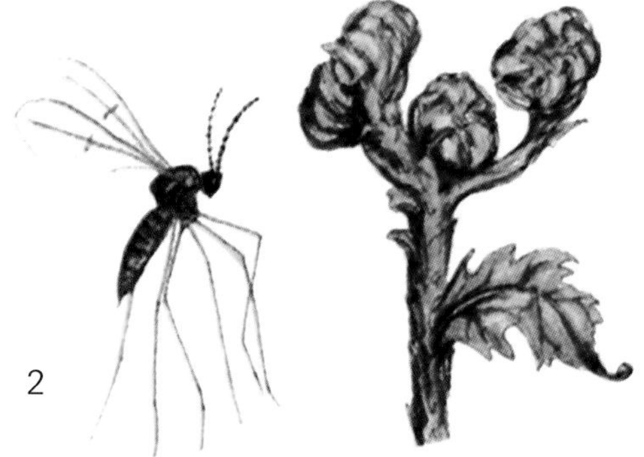

Other Midges

Biting Midges

Over 150 species in Britain. Tiny flies, up to 5 mm long, with small heads and quite long legs. Wings relatively large and folded flat at rest. Females bite, males have feathery antennae. May occur in large numbers, especially near northern streams and coasts. Larvae slender and worm-like; aquatic, in ponds or ditches, or terrestrial, often beneath bark of trees. Many adults prey on insects but some bite people, like *Culicoides pulicaris* (**4**). Most annoying on sultry summer evenings; bites cause much irritation.

4 

Other Midges

Owl Midges (1)

About 75 species in Britain. Tiny hairy flies like small moths, about 5 mm. The wings are broad and often held in a roof-like position over the back when the insect is at rest. They are weak fliers, and most often seen in windows, especially near drains or sewers, or on tree-trunks in damp shady places. Tiny, whitish larvae are semi-aquatic; they feed on decaying plant or animal remains or detritus in drains, sinks and sewers.

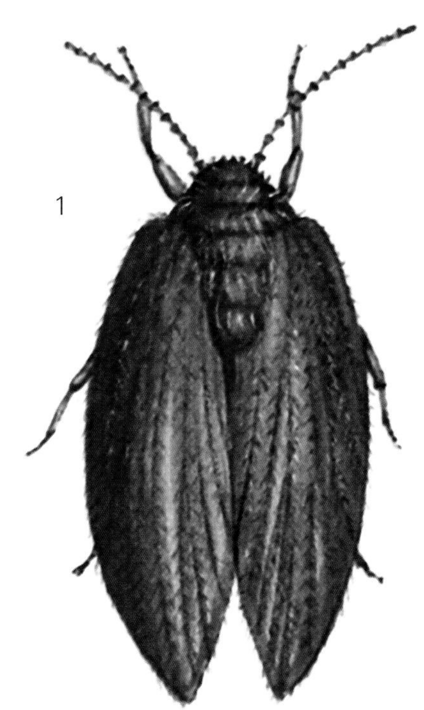

Other Midges

Black Flies

About 40 species in Britain. Very small, stout, black or grey flies, up to 5 mm long, with short thick legs, short antennae, humped backs and proportionately large wings with broad bases. Females bite horses, cattle and people, males do not bite. Common near running water, can be tormenting in sultry weather, swarming around the head and eyes. Larvae (**2**) are attached to rocks in fast-flowing water. *Simulium equinum* (**3**) is one of many similar species; it is most common near hill streams.

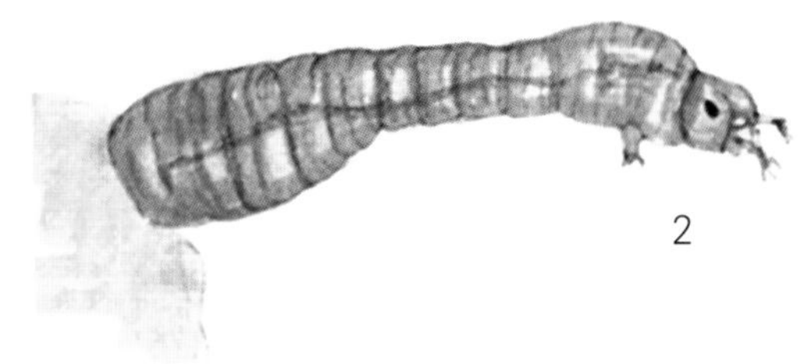

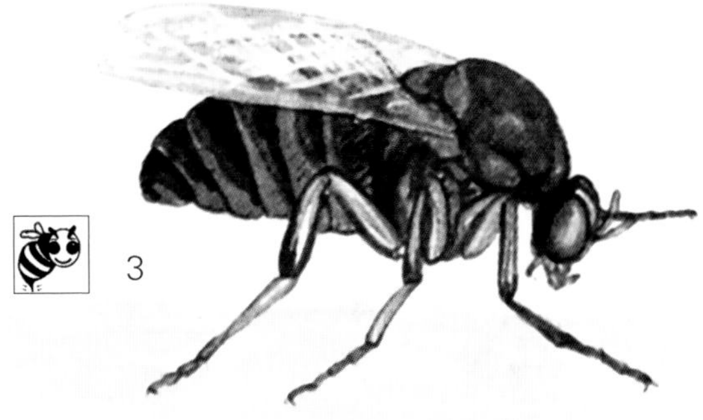

Crane Flies

About 300 species in Britain

Length: up to 32 mm; wingspan to 65 mm

Adult Characteristics

Long-legged flies (daddy-long-legs), with thin bodies and narrow wings, clumsy in movement and in flight. Their delicate legs break off easily. There is a prominent V-shaped line on the thorax between the wings. They do not bite.

Adult Biology

Abundant in a wide variety of habitats from grassland to woods, marshes and gardens; some come into houses. Most common in damp areas where larvae are abundant in the soil.

Larvae Characteristics and Biology

Many larvae live in soil, feeding on decaying plants or on roots of grasses and other plants; others live in leaf litter, decaying wood or water. Soil forms are called leatherjackets (**1**) and may be pests of farms and gardens but provide food for birds.

Common Species

Many are mosquito-size but the larger ***Tipula paludosa*** (**2**) is a common species, its leatherjackets found in meadows and lawns; adults fly to house lights in late summer. ***Tipula maxima*** is even larger with spotted wings. The similar **Winter Gnats** belong to another family; they appear in swarms in winter and spring.

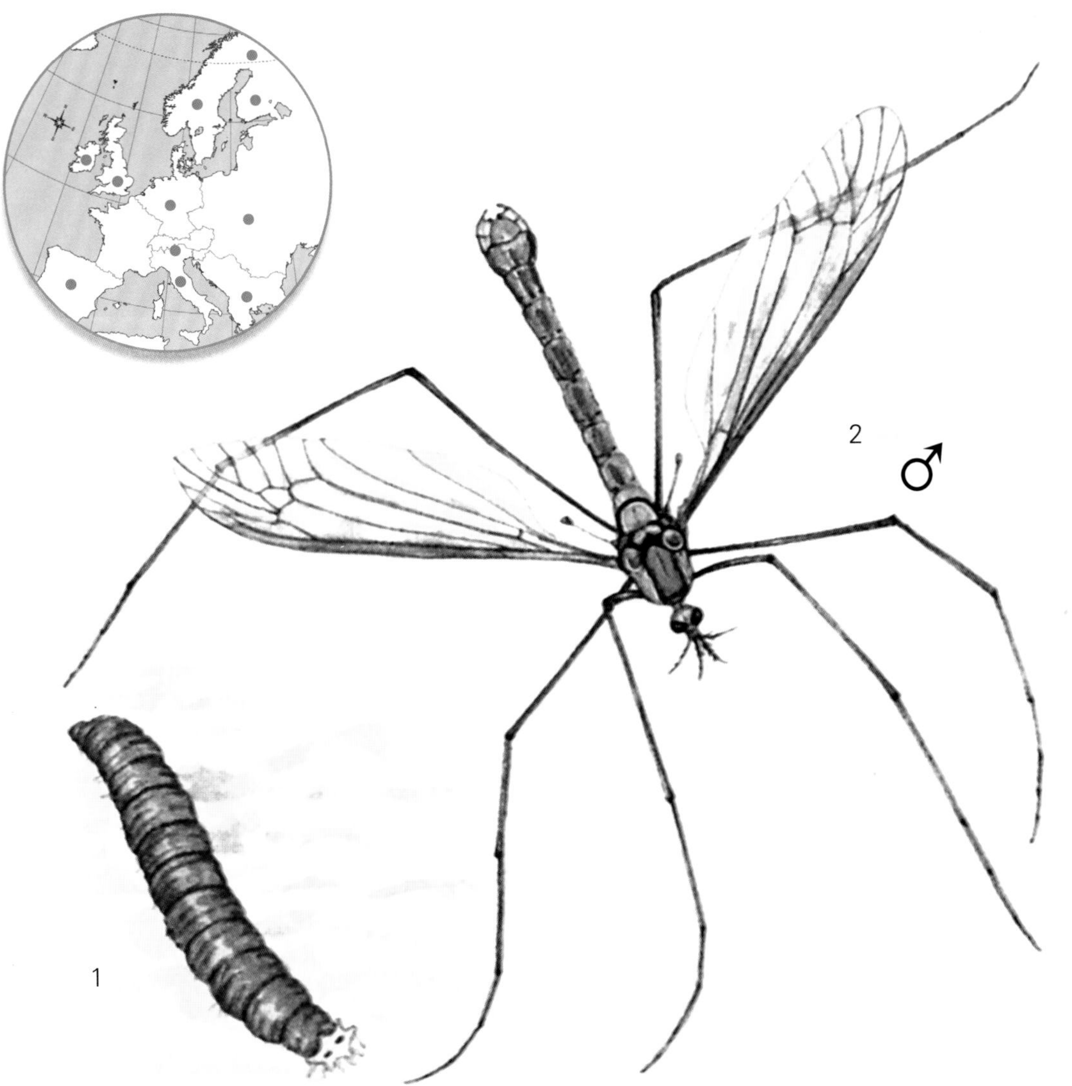

2
♂
1

Crane Flies are better known as Daddy-Long-Legs. Although they are quite large for an insect (wingspan up to 65 mm) they are harmless.

Soldier Flies

Over 50 species in Britain

Length: up to 20 mm

Adult Characteristics

Stout to slender, bristleless flies; most metallic or brightly coloured, some wasp-like. Abdomen flattened and often wider than folded wings. Wings folded neatly over each other, with parallel outside edges, when at rest. Each foot has three pads.

Adult Biology

Rather lazy flies, most often seen basking in sunshine on leaves and flowers, especially on members of the carrot family. Larger ones are slow, poor fliers but the slender *Sargus* species hover.

Larvae Characteristics and Biology

Larvae variable in their habits. Many are aquatic (**1**), others live in damp soil, decaying wood, fungi or rotting plant debris. Some feed on plant material, others are carnivores. They are often parasitized by chalcid wasps.

Common Species

Stratiomys chamaeleon (**2**) is one of the largest species; it is most often seen near water or in marshy areas of Europe and southern Britain; its larvae are aquatic. ***Chloromyia formosa*** (**3**) is smaller and more common, found in gardens and damp places; its larvae live in rotten wood or decaying plant material.

1
2
3

Robber Flies

27 species in Britain

Length: up to 30 mm

Adult Characteristics

Strong, medium-sized to large, bristly flies, with long bristly legs and narrow bodies. Feet have two pads at most. Eyes very large and separated by a deep groove, on a broad, flattened head. Face bearded with a piercing proboscis; they may bite if handled.

Adult Biology

Adults hunt insects like grasshoppers, wasps, bees. Some have a favourite perch and 'fly-jump' out at victims, others patrol on the wing. Prey collapse when bitten, probably poisoned.

Larvae Characteristics and Biology

Larvae (**1**) are cylindrical in form with two long hairs on each side of the thorax. They live in the soil, under bark or decaying wood or in leaves, and feed on rotting plant material.

Common Species

One of the largest European flies (and the largest British one) is *Asilus crabroniformis* (**2**), found in dry chalk grassland, pine woods and heaths. It waits for its prey on logs or on the ground. ***Dioctria rufipes*** (**3**) is common in summer meadows and hedgerows; it and several related flies catch prey in flight.

2

1

3

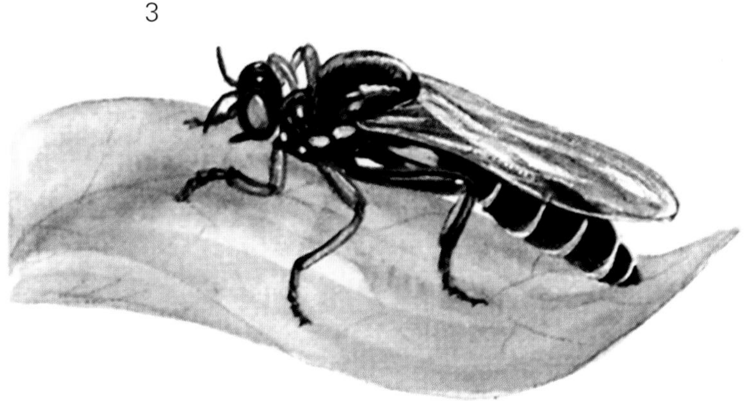

Robber Flies hunt for food, flying out at their victims, then biting, and probably poisoning, them. Here, however, two Robber Flies are seen mating.

Horse Flies

28 species in Britain

Length: up to 25 mm

Adult Characteristics

Quite large, robust, bristleless flies, with large heads and bulging, iridescent eyes. The feet have three pads. Antennae short and stout. Females have strong, piercing mouthparts and bite people, horses, cattle and deer.

Adult Biology

Females inflict painful bites. They fly swiftly and are most active in warm weather in summer and autumn. Males feed on nectar and are not often seen.

Larvae Characteristics and Biology

Larvae (**1**) large, rounded in cross-section and pointed at both ends. Found in damp places, in decaying logs, in soil, under stones or in water. Predaceous, hunting worms and insect larvae.

Common Species

Members of this family are most often found in old forested areas and pastures, often around horses and cattle. **Horse Flies** or Gad Flies (**2**) are large, up to 25 mm; they fly with a deep hum. **Clegs** (**3**) attack silently, their bite often the first sign of their presence. They seem to be most active in sultry weather.

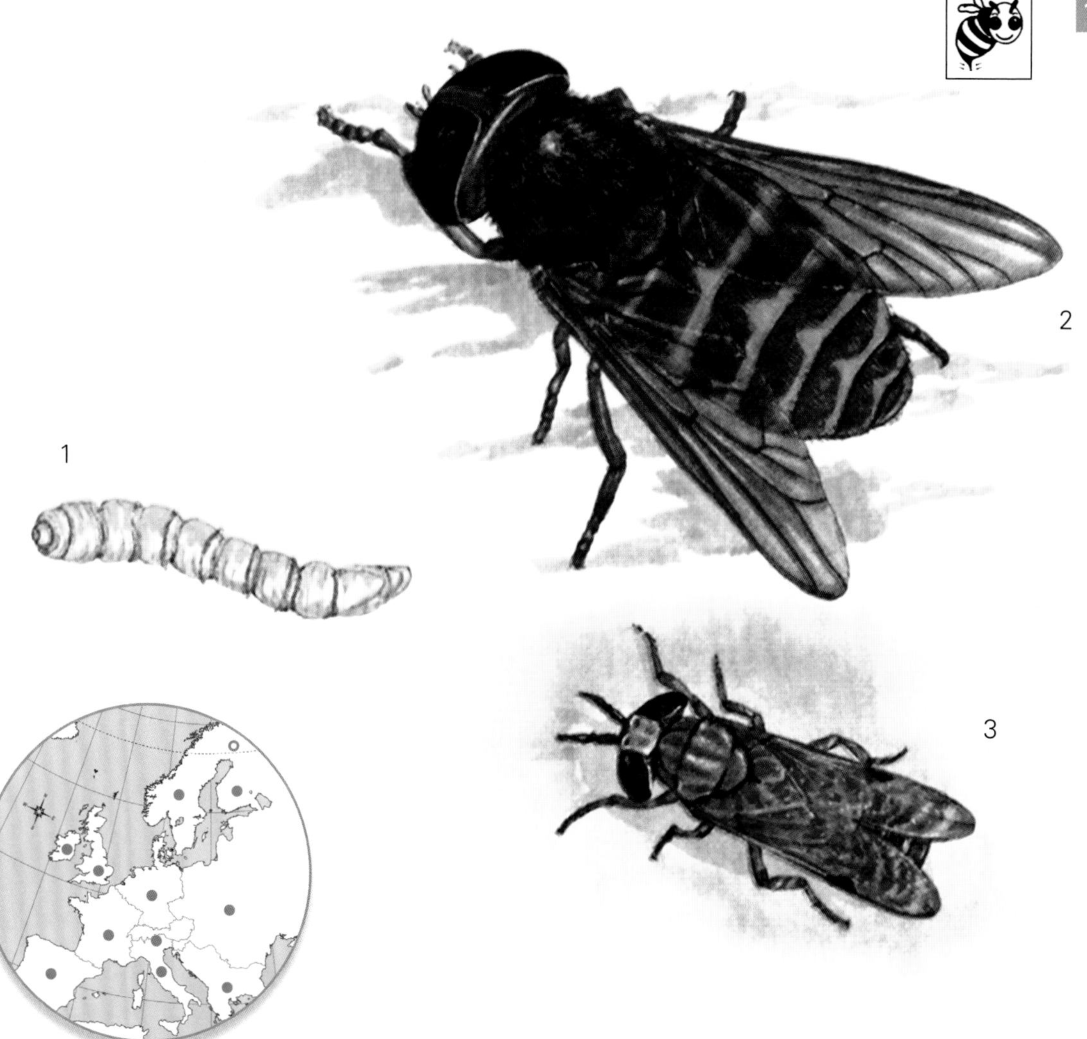
1
2
3

Hover Flies

Nearly 250 species in Britain

Length: 5–20 mm

Adult Characteristics

Small to large, bristleless flies, often striped in black and yellow or resembling bees. They have a distinctive false vein on each wing that does not link up with any other vein. The large eyes occupy a large part of the head. Proboscis short and fleshy.

Adult Biology

Quick, active flies that dart from place to place or hover in mid air. Usually seen around flowers where they feed on pollen and nectar; they are important pollinators.

Larvae Characteristics and Biology

Many larvae feed on aphids (**1**) and scale insects; others are aquatic, like rat-tailed maggots; some live in rotting wood; others in nests of bees, wasps and ants; a few attack bulbs. They look like tiny slugs with a pointed front end.

Common Species

Many species, like ***Syrphus ribesi*** (**3**), mimic **wasps** or **bees** (deterring would-be predators); they are harmless. **Drone Flies** (**4**), adults of rat-tailed maggots, resemble honey bee drones, ***Volucella bombylans*** resembles a bumble bee. Distinguished from wasps and bees by their hovering or darting flight.

1
4
3
2

Hover Flies are important pollinators, as they feed on pollen and nectar.

Bot and Warble Flies

Length: 10–15 mm

5 species in Britain

Adult Characteristics

Stout, softly hairy flies, with a swelling on the thorax and a fan of hairs behind the balancing organ (like parasitic flies). Mouthparts are vestigial and adult flies do not feed.

Adult Biology

Adult females fly around cattle or sheep laying their eggs on the legs of cattle, or the noses of sheep. They cause distress or even panic in the animals who try desperately to avoid them.

Larvae Characteristics and Biology

Larvae are parasitic. They develop in sheep or cattle. They all cause considerable, and sometimes serious, loss of condition in the animals.

Common Species

Warble Flies (1) lay eggs on the legs of cattle; larvae migrate to the backs of the animals and there cause inflamed swellings (warbles). Larvae of **Sheep-Bot Flies (2)** develop in the sheep nostrils, causing considerable distress. **Horse-Bot Flies (3)** are more like house flies; larvae develop in intestines of horses.

1
2
3

Parasitic Flies

Over 250 species in Britain

Length: 4–20 mm

Adult Characteristics

Large, stout, dull-coloured flies with many large bristles, especially on the back of the abdomen. They have a large swelling on the thorax, best seen from the side of the fly, and a fan of bristles behind the balancing organ. They are strong fliers.

Adult Biology

Adults are found in a wide variety of habitats from meadows, fields and gardens to woods and forests. They visit flowers to feed on nectar and pollen.

Larvae Characteristics and Biology

Larvae live as parasites inside insects like beetle and sawfly larvae, caterpillars, nymphs of grasshoppers and bugs. Eggs are laid on leaves to be eaten by caterpillars or laid on or inserted into the host. Larvae develop inside the living host.

Common Species

Along with parasitic wasps, these flies are largely responsible for controlling insect populations. ***Tachina grossa*** (**1**) resembles a bumble bee; it is the largest fly in this family in Europe, found in woods and heaths. Its larvae develop in caterpillars. Larvae of ***Dexia rustica*** (**2**) develop in larvae of chafer beetles.

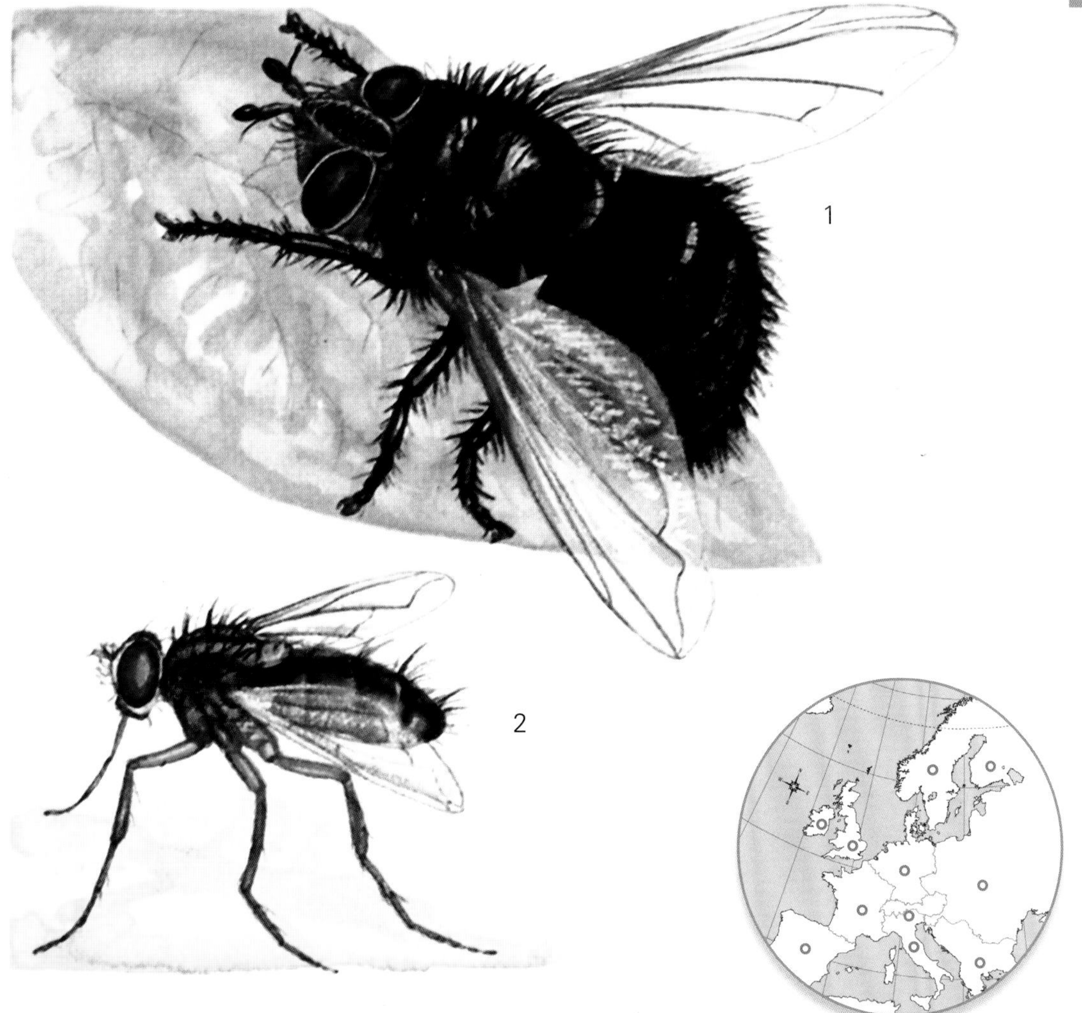
1
2

Blow Flies

Over 90 species in Britain

Length: 5–15 mm

Adult Characteristics

Metallic blue, green or black, bristly flies with a large lobe at the base of each wing. There is no swelling on the thorax such as is seen in Parasitic Flies but there is a fan of bristles behind the balancing organ. These flies buzz loudly in flight.

Adult Biology

Adults feed on rotting plants and carrion and are often found in large numbers around such materials. Females attracted to fresh meat and open wounds. Males, especially, also feed on pollen.

Larvae Characteristics and Biology

Most larvae (**1**) develop from eggs laid in carrion, in dung, or around wounds in living animals. They will also develop in meat or wounds if allowed, keeping the wound sterile but unhealed.

Common Species

Bluebottles (**2**) are household and farmyard pests, coming into houses, laying eggs on exposed meat and other foods. **Greenbottles** (**3**) are more often found outside, laying eggs on carrion and dung. The related **Flesh Flies** are greyish black with red eyes; females deposit developing larvae (not eggs) on carrion.

2

1

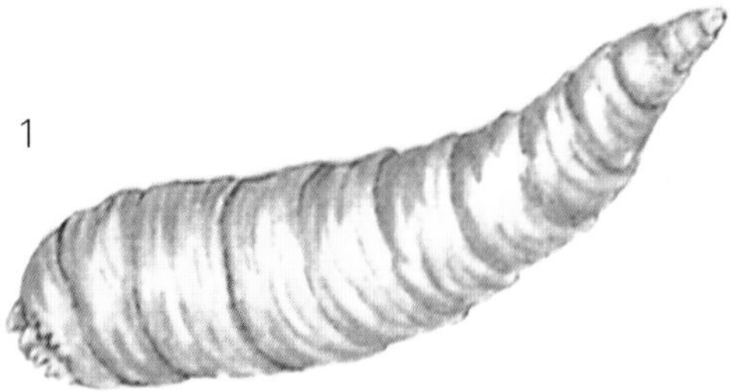

3

Greenbottles lay their eggs on carrion and dung. They are a species of Blow Fly, of which there are over 90 in Britain.

House Flies

About 500 species in Britain

Length: up to 12 mm

Adult Characteristics

Stout, active flies, usually grey or brown, sometimes black or yellow, with a broad lobe at the base of each wing. Although they are generally bristly, there is no fan of bristles behind the balancing organ.

Adult Biology

Many adults are found around houses and farms, where they feed on dung and excreta, nectar and exposed foods. Others found in woods, on tree-trunks; still others on sea-shores.

Larvae Characteristics and Biology

Larvae (**1**) of many species develop in decaying vegetation, manure and dung, also in carrion and garbage. Others attack living plants.

Common Species

Common House Flies (**2**) are vectors for several diseases like typhoid, dysentery, cholera and worms, which they carry on their feet. **Lesser House Flies** (**3**) spend their time circling around lights and other objects in houses and restaurants. Neither of these species bite.

1
2
3
4

House Flies

Many other familiar flies are members of this family. **Sweat Flies** (**4** on facing page) gather around the heads of walkers in woods, or around cattle; they are attracted to sweat which they sip. **Stable Flies** (**1**) are found around farms and fields; they bite. Their larvae develop in piles of decaying straw, vegetation and manure. The furry, golden-yellow flies most often seen on cow-pats are male **Yellow Dung Flies** (**2**); they are waiting for the grey-green, less furry females, which come to lay their eggs in the dung.

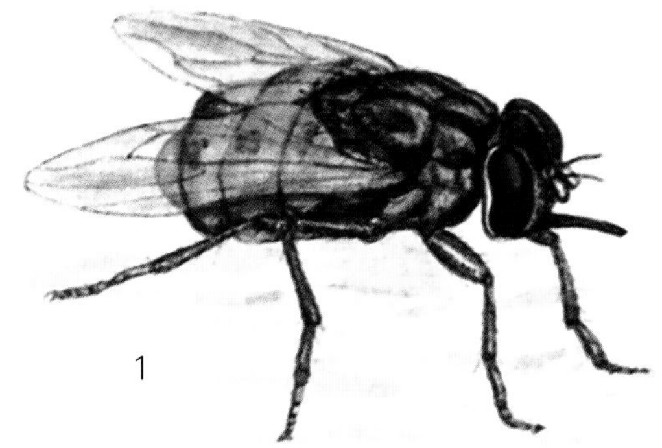

1

2

House Flies

Root and Seed Maggots

A subfamily of house flies, with 150 British species of slender, dark flies. They have relatively long legs. Many of their larvae (or maggots) feed on decaying plants or fungi, but others attack living plants. Some are pests. The maggots of **Onion Flies** (**3**) attack onions (**4**); Cabbage Root Fly maggots attack roots of cabbages, cauliflowers etc; larvae of Wheat Bulb Flies attack cereals.

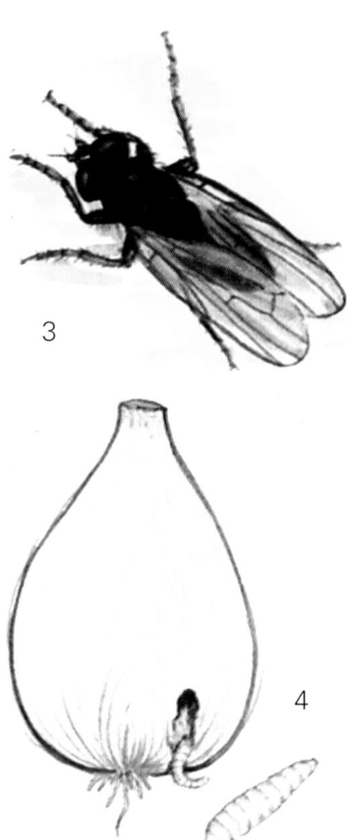

Yellow Dung Flies are the flies that you are most likely to see on a cowpat. The males are yellow and the females grey-green.

Other Flies

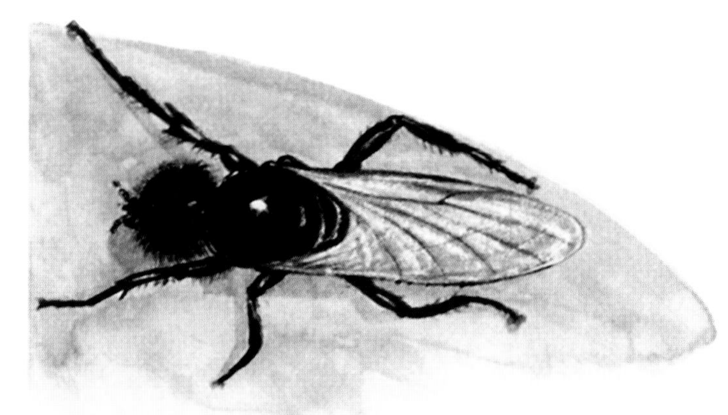

March Flies

Eighteen species in Britain. Black hairy flies with short stout antennae inserted below the eyes. Adults most common in grassy places in spring. **St Mark's Fly** (**1**) is the largest species (up to 13 mm long); it appears around St Mark's Day (25 April). Males fly slowly, with legs hanging, looking for females which sit in the grass. Fever Fly is similar but smaller; it behaves in a similar way. Larvae live in the soil and feed on roots.

Other Flies

Dance Flies

Over 300 species in Britain. Small- and medium-sized, bristly flies, up to 12 mm long, with more or less spherical heads on slender necks. Legs often thickened. Proboscis rigid and piercing, directed downward in many species; used for sucking juices from other insects, mainly flies. Adults often congregate in dancing swarms, like gnats. Larvae live in soil, rotting wood or in water. ***Emphis tessellata*** (**2**) is a large species, often seen on flowers of hawthorn or members of carrot family.

Other Flies

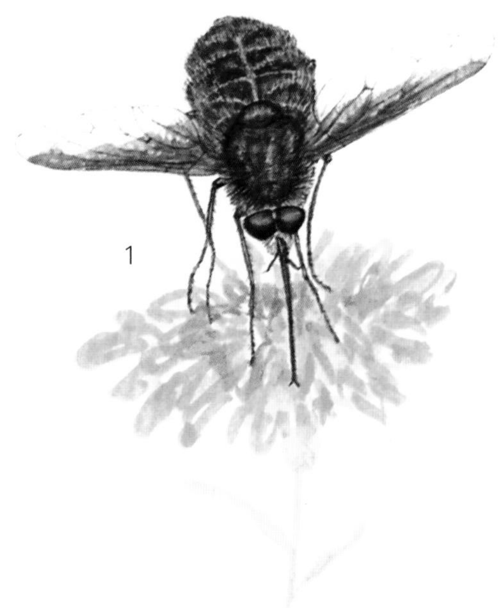

Bee Flies

About 12 species in Britain. Stout, furry flies, up to 12 mm long, like active bumble bees. They have long, thin legs and proboscis-like mouthparts but do not bite. Wings held outstretched at rest. Flies hover motionless except for rapid wing vibration, darting away if disturbed. Seen above bare ground, around flowers, resting on leaves or on the ground. Larvae are parasites on other insects, caterpillars, bees, wasps and other flies. **Common Bee Fly** (**1**) is common in Europe and southern England.

Other Flies

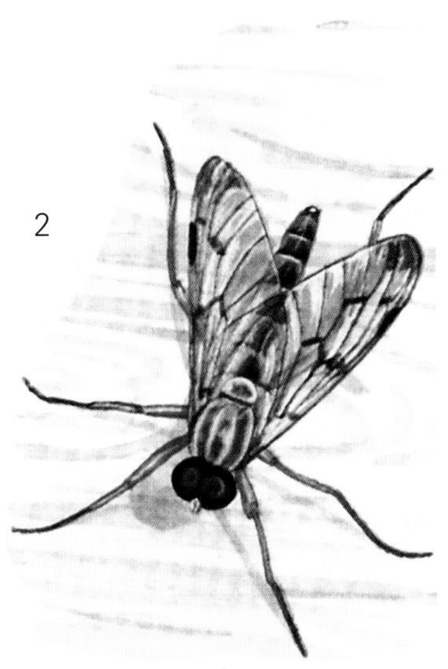

Snipe Flies

Eighteen species in Britain. Small to fairly large flies, with slender bodies and long legs. Often yellow and brown in colour. Their feet have three pads. The large **Snipe Fly** (**2**) itself (up to 18 mm long) is found in wooded areas, males usually resting head down on tree trunks or fences, or making sudden darting flights. Its larvae are long and whitish, found in soil or leaf litter, feeding on insects and other small animals.

The Common Bee Fly has a resemblance to a bee or wasp which will be useful for laying its eggs on other species' caterpillars.

Other Flies

Long-Legged Flies

Over 250 species in Britain. Small, bristly flies, up to 7 mm long, with long legs. Often metallic green or blue in colour. Common in damp places near water, in wet meadows, marshes and along streams, even skating on the water or on mud. Adults and larvae are carnivores, hunting small insects. Larvae live in wet places. *Poecilobothrus nobilitatus* (**1**) is common around ponds, especially those covered in duckweed. It is one of many species in the family, whose males have large, very ornamental sex organs.

Other Flies

Shore Flies and Kelp Flies

There are about 120 species of **Shore Flies** (**2**) in Britain, small dark flies, up to 8 mm long; they may be present in large numbers on the water surface at edges of ponds, streams and marshes, or on the coast. They feed on other insects trapped in the water film.

The seven species of **Kelp Flies** (**3**) are flattened, bristly flies, up to 8 mm long. They are found, often in large numbers, on flowers near the coast or in stranded seaweed on coastal beaches.

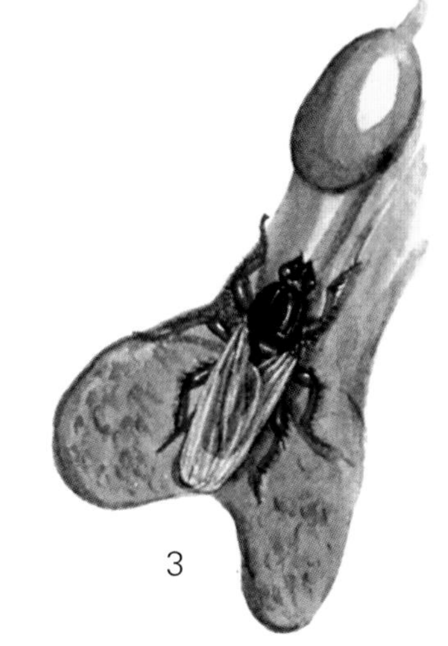

Fruit Flies

Fruit Gall Flies

Over 70 species in Britain. Small flies, about 5 mm long, with elaborate patterns on wings; females have pointed abdomens and rigid ovipositors. Males sit on leaves, opening and closing their wings, courting the females. Larvae are white maggots found in flowers, fruits or stems of many plants; some are crop pests, like the Celery Fly and Mediterranean Fruit Fly. Many make galls, especially in flowers of the daisy family. The larvae of **Thistle Gall-Flies** (**1**) make stem galls in Field and Spear Thistles (**2**).

Fruit Flies

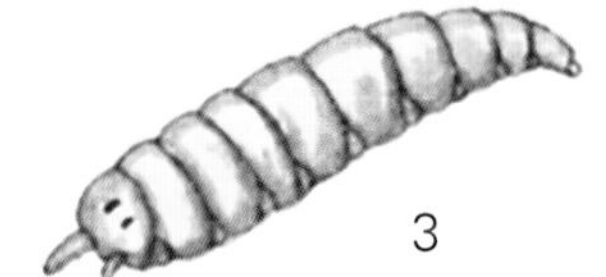

Vinegar Flies

Over 50 species in Britain. Small flies, about 5 mm long, often found around rotting and fermenting fruit, in restaurants, jam factories, breweries, pubs etc. They feed on yeasts, also on flower nectar and sap. Larvae (**3**) are whitish maggots which burrow into fermenting fruit or fungi, feeding on yeasts and bacteria. The yellow and brown **Laboratory Fruit Flies** (**4**) are not only common in the wild (with many similar species) but are also used in studies on heredity.

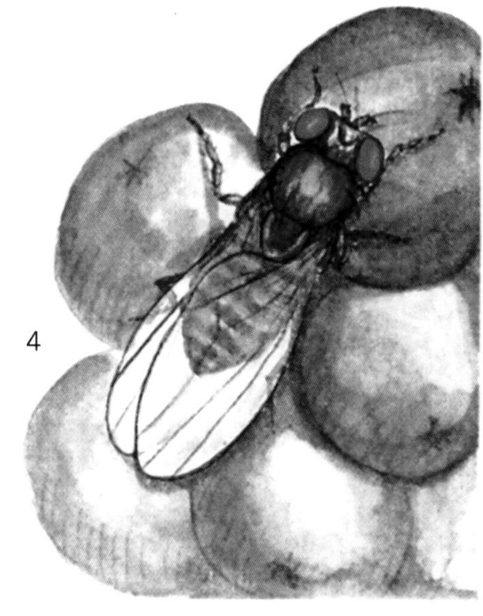

Beetles

4000 species in Britain

Length: usually 0.5–25 mm

Adult Characteristics

Distinctive insects with horny or leathery fore wings called elytra which meet in a straight line in the centre of the back. Hind wings membranous and used for flying; they are folded under elytra when insect is at rest. Antennae usually have 11 segments.

Adult Biology

Beetles may be aquatic, some live in wood, others in fungi or on flowers and leaves; some are household pests. They have biting mouthparts; many feed on plants, others hunt insects, slugs etc.

Larvae Characteristics and Biology

Larva has well-developed hard head, a thorax and a soft or hard abdomen. Active predaceous forms have well-developed legs and antennae, soil and wood-boring forms are often legless and grub-like with soft bodies.

Common Species

Largest order of animals with over 300,000 species in the world. Illustrated on this page are the **Pea Weevil** (**1**), whose larvae develop in peas; a **Cardinal Beetle**, seen on old trees and flowers (**2**); ***Byrrhus pilula*** (**3**), which plays dead if disturbed; and ***Oncomera femorata*** (**4**), often seen on flowers.

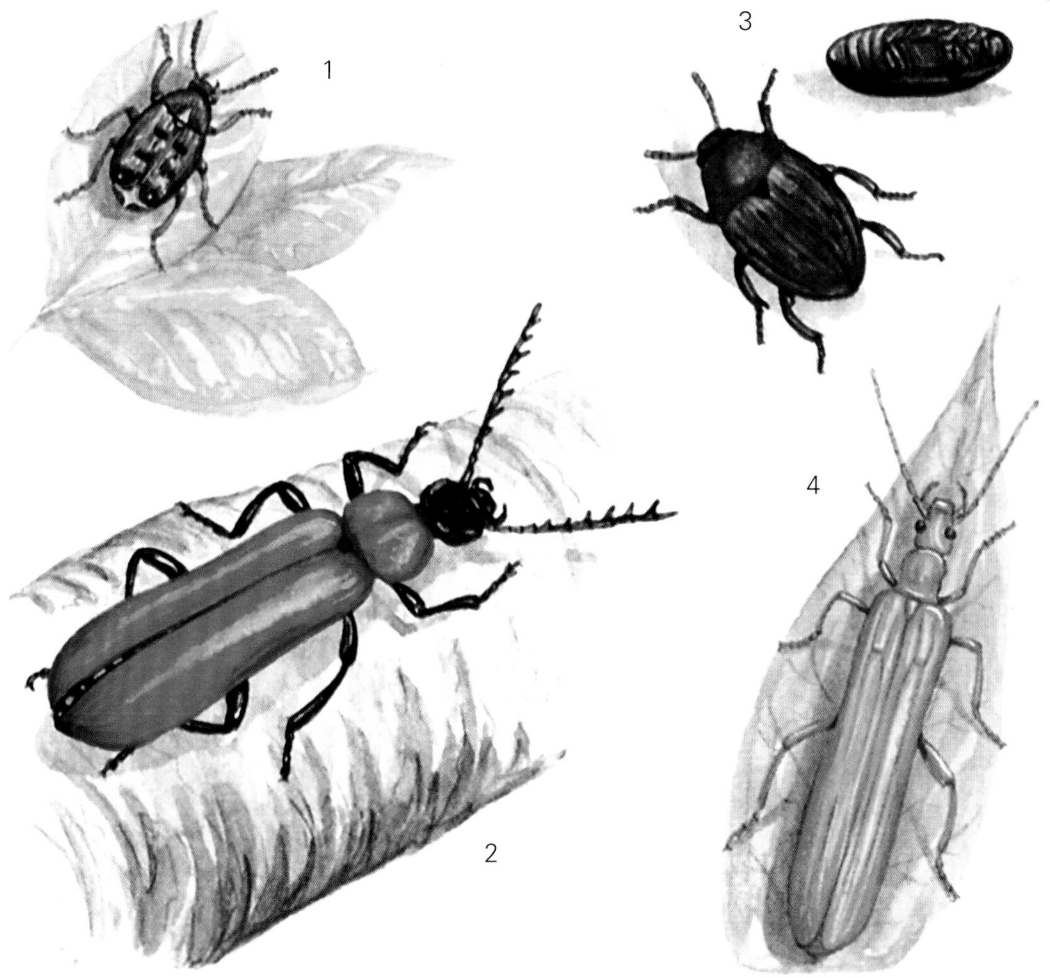
1
2
3
4

The Cardinal Beetle, so called because its red colour is usually seen on old trees and on flowers.

Darkling Beetles

About 35 species in Britain

Length: 3–30 mm

Adult Characteristics

Hard-bodied, oval or oblong beetles, often awkward and slow-moving. Most are black or dark brown, some with red markings; many have striated or roughened elytra. Antennae are thread-like or bead-like; their origin on the head cannot be seen from above.

Adult Biology

Usually nocturnal. A diverse group, living in decaying plants or fungi, under bark or leaves, in cellars. Some are pests of stored food. Many are flightless, their elytra fastened down.

Larvae Characteristics and Biology

Larvae are scavengers like many adults, living in similar places and feeding on similar foods. They are shiny and cylindrical, their form typified by the mealworms (**1**), pests in stored grains but also used as food for pet amphibians and reptiles.

Common Species

Mealworm adult (**2**), and the similar but smaller and lighter Flour Beetles, are found in flour in stores and mills. The large **Churchyard Beetle** (**3**) is one of the flightless species; it lives in cellars and caves and emits a foul scent if disturbed.

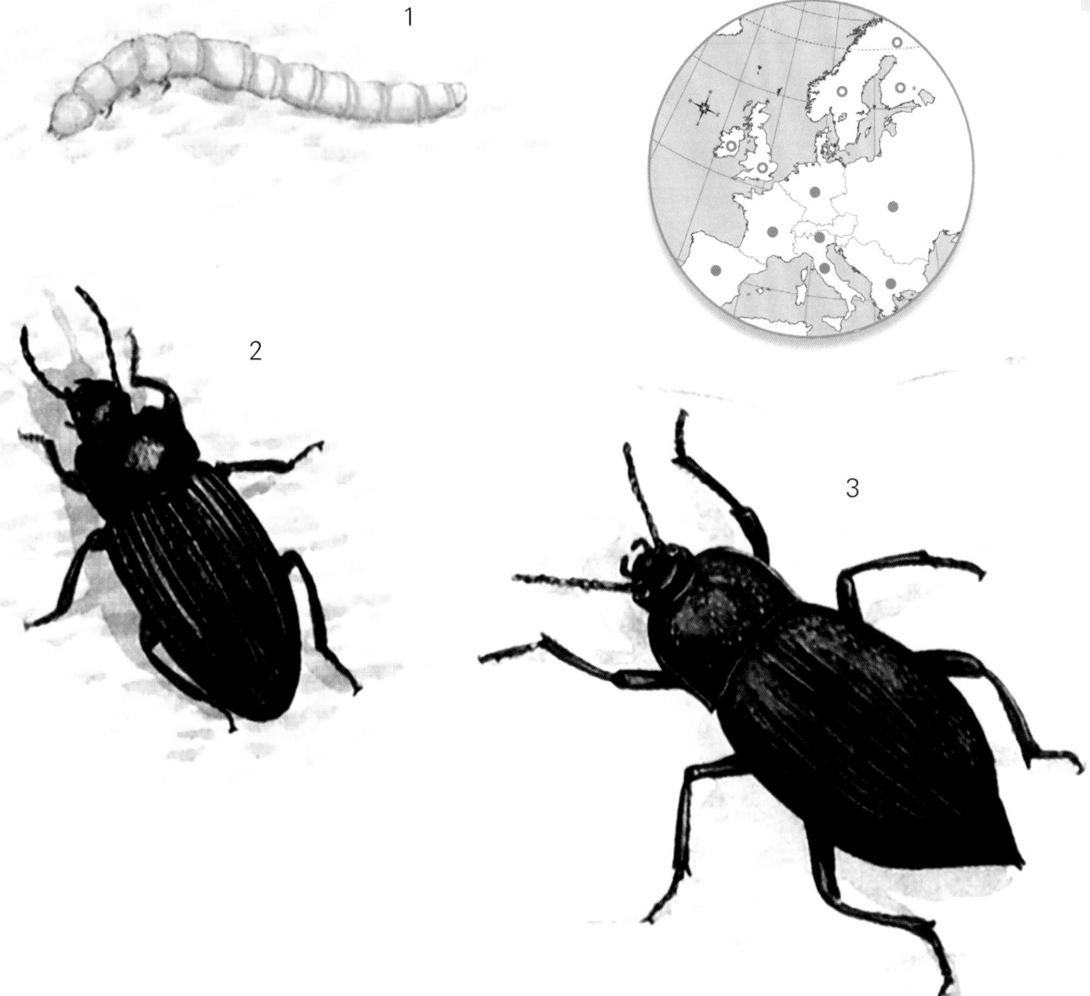
1
2
3

Tiger Beetles

About 5 species in Britain

Length: 8–20 mm

Adult Characteristics

Fast-moving beetles with elongated, cylindrical bodies and long legs. Many are metallic green or brown with lighter patterns. Head and eyes large, as wide as pronotum, but narrower than elytra; antennae thread-like, attached to top of head.

Adult Biology

Active by day. Found mainly in dry sandy places, in woods and heaths. Active hunters, moving fast and often flying for short distances if disturbed. They may bite if handled incautiously.

Larvae Characteristics and Biology

Larvae (**1**) long, whitish grubs with large heads and powerful jaws. They live in vertical burrows in the ground, waiting at top of burrow for prey (other insects) to venture close and then seizing them.

Common Species

Green Tiger Beetle (**2**) is found in sandy places, heaths, dunes and woodland paths in summer, throughout Europe and Britain. Wood Tiger Beetle is bronze, iridescent green or violet on the underside; it lives in sandy pine woods and heaths in northern and central Europe but is rare in Britain.

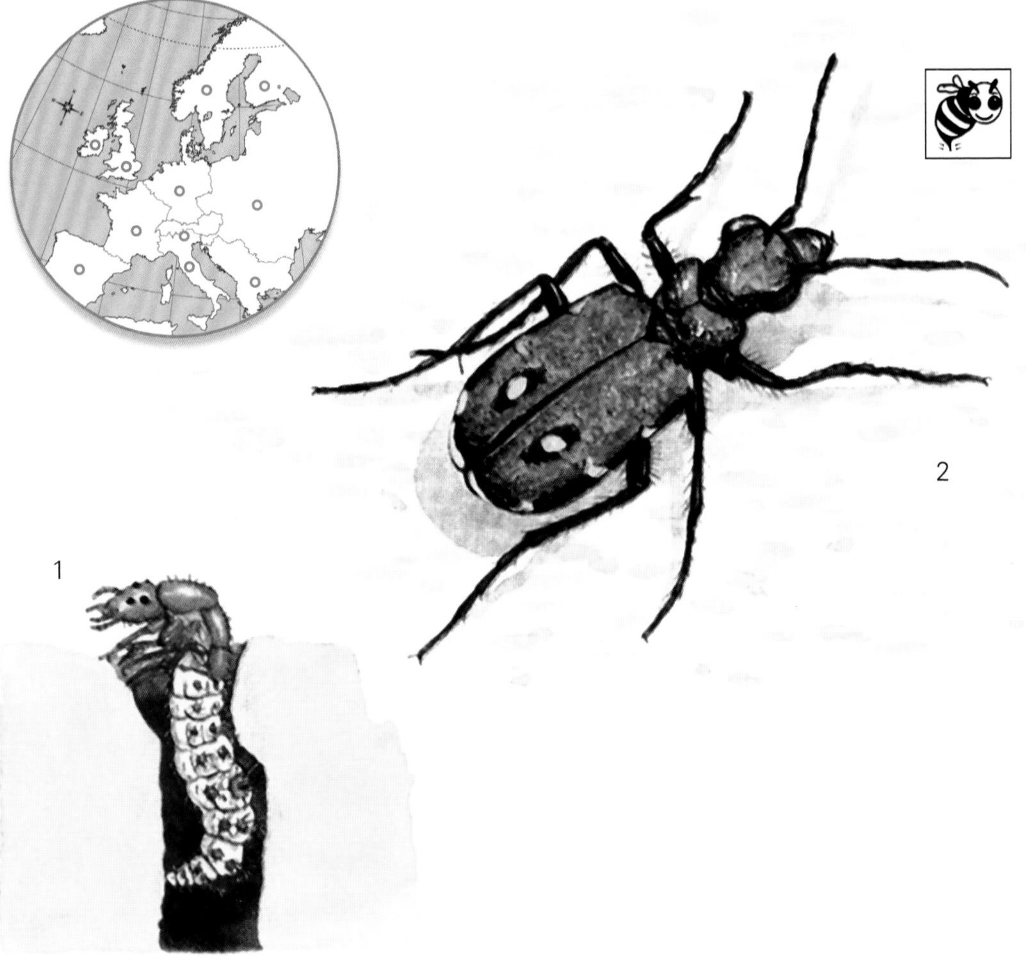
1
2

The Green Tiger Beetle is found in dunes and heaths throughout Europe and Britain. It has a striking metallic green body and the larvae are whitish.

Ground Beetles

About 350 species in Britain

Length: 1–60 mm

Adult Characteristics

Elongated, rather flattened beetles with long legs which have spurs. Mostly black, but some are brightly coloured or metallic. Often pronotum narrower than elytra and head small, narrower than pronotum. Antennae thread-like, attached to side of head.

Adult Biology

Mostly active at night. Adults rarely fly but can run fast, often hide under stones, debris or logs. Hunt prey, including pests like caterpillars and slugs; some also feed on plants or carrion.

Larvae Characteristics and Biology

Larvae (**1**) have long flattened bodies, well-developed legs and sharp jaws. They live in underground burrows or hide in similar places to adults. They are active predators like adults.

Common Species

Violet Ground Beetles (**2**) hunt slugs in woods and gardens. **Bombardier Beetles** (**3**) spray toxic liquid from anal glands as a defence mechanism; several similar species occur in Europe, one in chalky areas of southern England. Black Beetles are very common in gardens, fields and cellars, often found under stones.

1
2
3

Violet Ground Beetles hunt slugs in woods and gardens. They are one of 350 species of Ground Beetle in Britain.

Rove Beetles

Nearly 1000 species in Britain

Length: 1–25 mm

Adult Characteristics

Slender, elongated, parallel-sided beetles with short elytra which leave most of the abdomen exposed. Abdomen flexible, often bent upwards, especially when disturbed. Often shiny but usually dull-coloured, often black. Antennae thread-like.

Adult Biology

Found on carrion, dung or fungi, decaying plant material or under stones, logs or debris, in wet places and ants' nests. Most are predators on other insects, can run fast and fly well.

Larvae Characteristics and Biology

Larvae (**1**) similar to adults but wingless. They are often predators like the adults and found in similar places.

Common Species

Devil's Coach-Horse (**2**) is found under stones and debris in gardens and woods; it is one of the largest rove beetles and raises its hind end when disturbed. ***Paederus littoralis*** (**3**) is a very small but strikingly coloured, flightless species; it lives in damp meadows and near water.

1
2
3

Sexton Beetles

60 species in Britain

Length: 4–25 mm

Adult Characteristics

Mainly dark, often large beetles, some with orange markings. They often have relatively soft and flattened bodies and the elytra are shortened so that the hind end of the abdomen is exposed. Antennae are clubbed.

Adult Biology

Many are found near bodies of mice, birds, etc., which they feed on; some bury the bodies. Others feed on rotting fungi or plants; some are predators. Most fly well and come to lights at night.

Larvae Characteristics and Biology

Many of the larvae feed on carrion like the adults. Larvae of Burying Beetles have three developmental forms, the first active with well-developed legs (**1**), the last almost maggot-like. Larvae of Carrion Beetles resemble woodlice.

Common Species

Common Burying Beetle (**2**) is one of several similar species; others are all black. Males and females find a body by its scent, and the first pair drive off late-comers; female lays eggs near the body and feeds the larvae at first.
Four-Spot Carrion Beetle (**3**) lives in oak woods; it feeds on moth caterpillars.

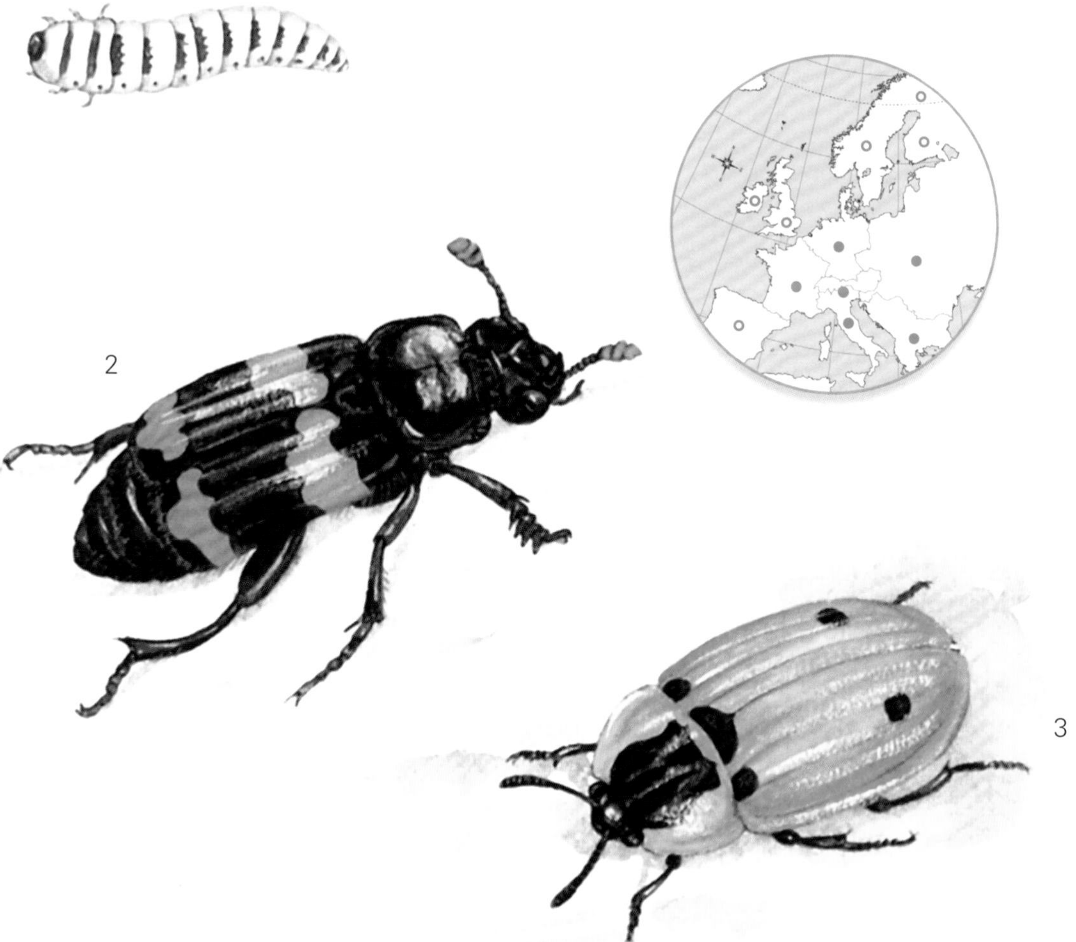
1
2
3

Scarab Beetles

About 90 species in Britain

Length: 3–40 mm

Adult Characteristics

Mostly short, stout, convex beetles, with large heads. The distinctive antennae are elbowed, with clubs formed of 7–11 leaf-like segments. The beetles vary in colour from dull brown to metallic green or blue and some have bright markings.

Adult Biology

Many adults feed on leaves, pollen, sap or fruits and are found on plants; some are pests on crops. Others feed on fungi, on rotting vegetation or on dung.

Larvae Characteristics and Biology

Larvae (**1**) are usually C-shaped with white bodies and brown heads. They live in a variety of habitats; many live in the soil and damage lawns and crops by feeding on roots, others live in dung, carrion, under bark and in rotting vegetation.

Common Species

A diverse family, including scarabs, dung beetles and chafers. **Cockchafers** or May Bugs (**2**) are one of the largest chafers; they fly in the evening in May and June. **Garden Chafers** (**3**) fly later in summer, often in dry grassy places or around shrubs. The green Rose Chafers fly around flowers, including roses.

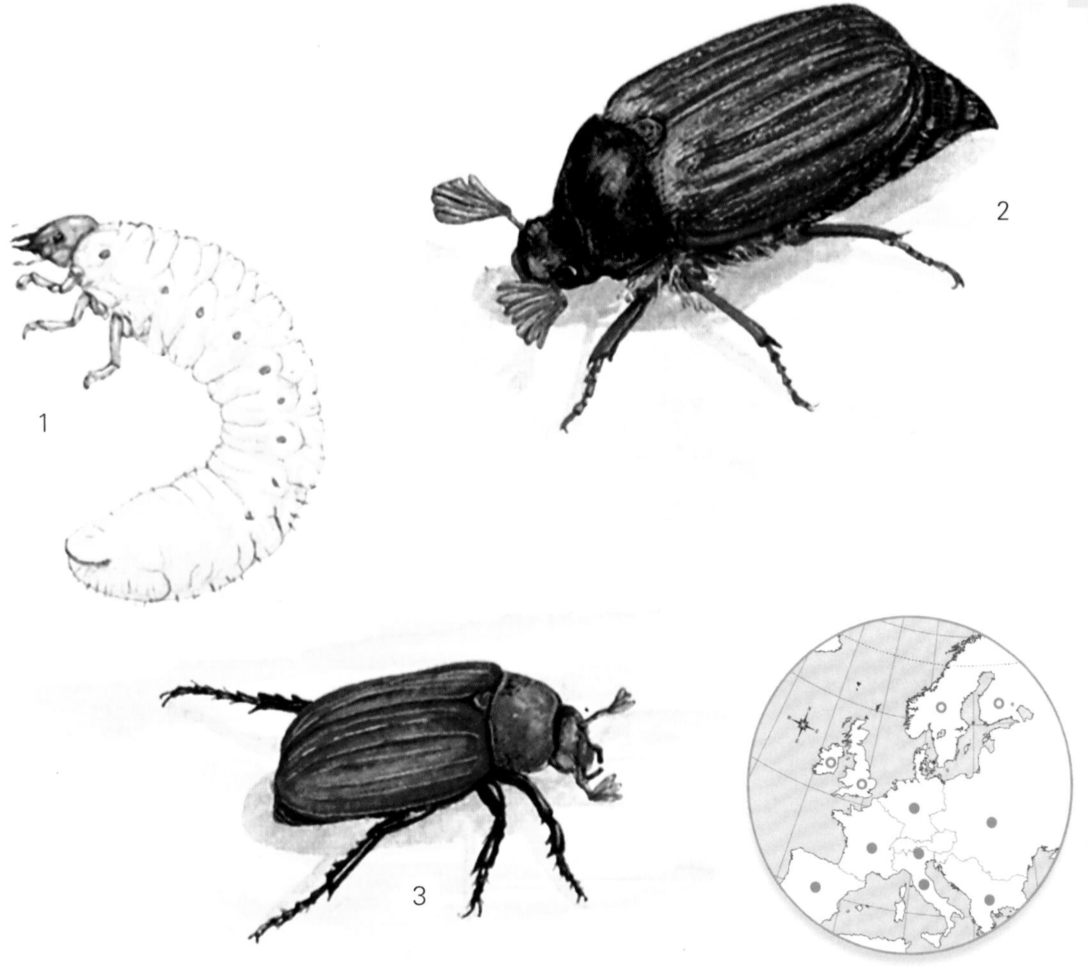
1
2
3

The Cockchafer is also known as a May Bug and is one of the largest species of Scarab Beetle in Britain.

Dung Beetles

Scarab Dung Beetles

Often black, bronze or green, and some males have horns. Found in or near the dung on which they feed. There are many **Aphodius** species in the meadows and pastures of Europe and Britain, including *A. fimitarius* (**1**) and the all-black **A. rufipes**. They are found in the dung of cows, sheep and horses. Both males and females of *Copris lunarius* (**2**) make burrows beneath cow dung, lay eggs in these burrows, then feed and guard the larvae until they are ready to leave.

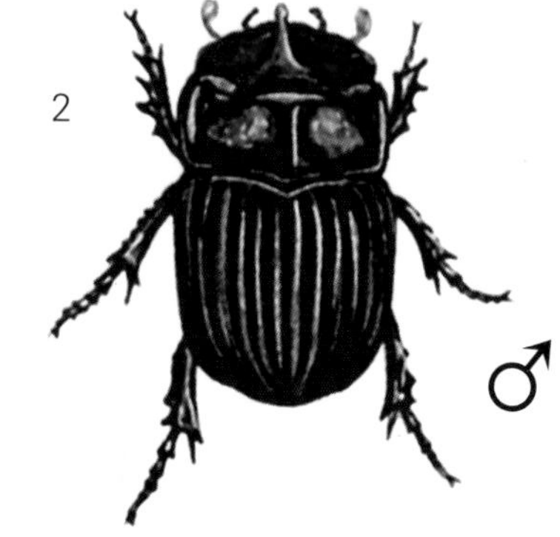

Dung Beetles

Dor Beetles

Eight species in Britain. Mostly large, black, often iridescent beetles, 10–25 mm long. Antennae end in three-jointed clubs. Front legs have powerful spines used for digging. Adults dig burrows beneath dung and haul balls of dung into the burrows. An egg is laid on the dung ball; both adults and larvae feed on dung. The **Lousy Watchman** (**3**) is common on cow dung or may be seen flying in the evening. It is often infested with mites.

Click Beetles

About 65 species in Britain

Length: 3–28 mm

Adult Characteristics

Distinctive beetles because of the way they can flip into the air if they fall on their backs. They turn over several times in the air and may land right way up; if not they flip again. They are flattened and elongated, usually dull, often brown or black.

Adult Biology

Adults live on leaves and flowers of herbaceous plants, in decaying wood or under bark. Many to do not feed at all while others feed on leaves, pollen or nectar.

Larvae Characteristics and Biology

Larvae are wireworms (**1**); hard-bodied, shiny, brown or yellow in colour, cylindrical in shape. Most live in soil, feeding on seeds or roots. Many are pests in fields of grains and other crops. Others are predators in decaying wood or under bark.

Common Species

Agriotes lineatus (**2**) is found in grassland and arable land, where its wireworm larvae often damage root crops. Other similar species live in woods and hedgerows. Some have large coloured spots on the elytra like ***Oedostethus 4-pustulatus*** (**3**), found under stones in grassy damp places.

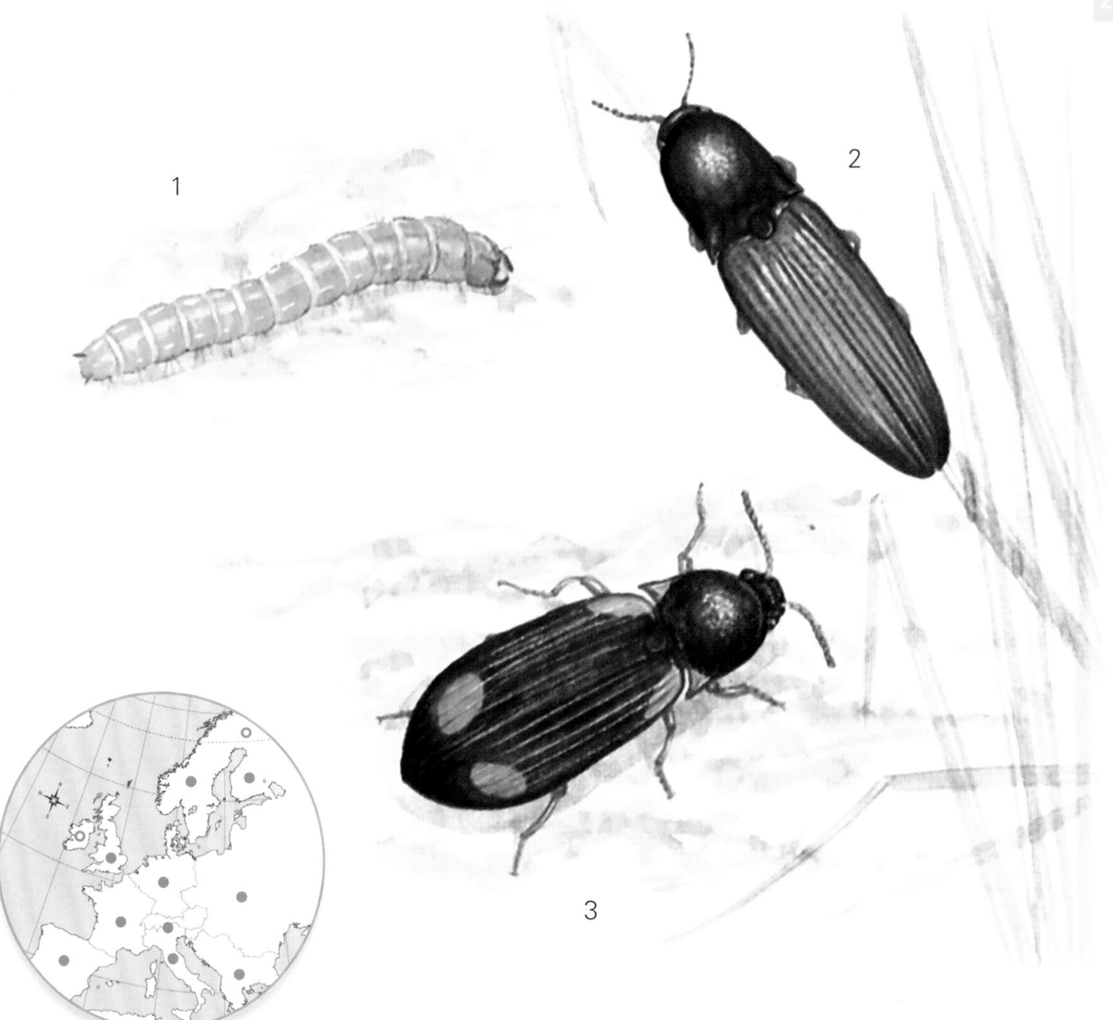
1
2
3

Click Beetles can flick themselves into the air if they land on their backs, and keep doing this until they land the right way up.

Soldier Beetles

About 40 species in Britain

Length: 3–15 mm

Adult Characteristics

Elongated, more or less parallel-sided, soft-bodied beetles with leathery, hairy elytra, softer than those of many beetles. Often reddish but the elytra may be black. The pronotum is not extended over the head.

Adult Biology

Found on flowers and leaves, especially on members of carrot and daisy families, also on blackberries; in hedgerows, woods and grassland. Predators, feeding on other insects. They fly well.

Larvae Characteristics and Biology

Larvae (**1**) appear velvety, with a dense covering of hairs and are often dark in colour. They are predators, living on the ground, beneath stones, in moss and debris, where they catch soft-bodied insects, like caterpillars and fly maggots, or slugs and snails.

Common Species

Soldier Beetles (**2**) are common on flowers and shrubs; they are also known as Bloodsuckers because of their colour, but are harmless. There are several similar, but larger species. Others have yellow or black elytra, like ***Cantharis rustica*** (**3**).

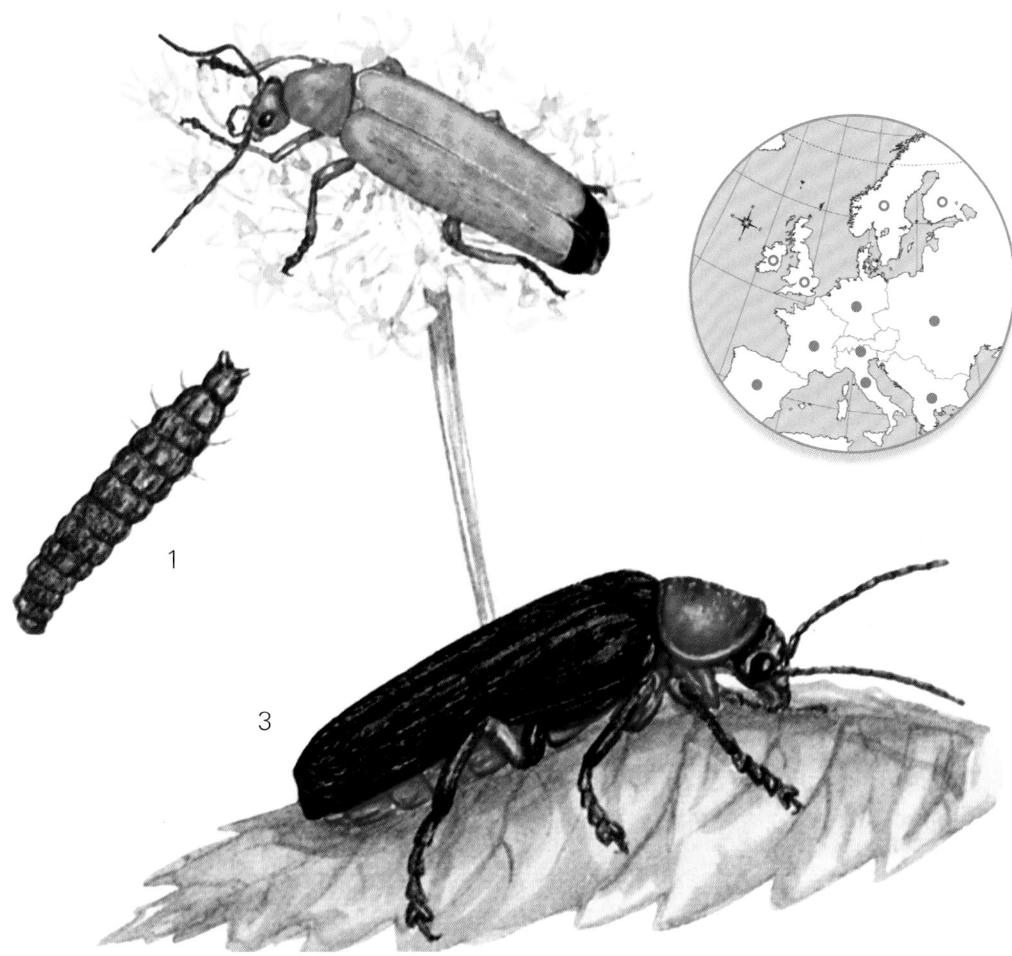
2
1
3

Soldier Beetles are sometimes known as Bloodsuckers because of their colouring. However they will not bite, although they do feed on larvae.

Death Watch and Furniture Beetles

Length: 2–5 mm

About 28 species in Britain

Adult Characteristics

Small, dark-brown to black beetles, often elongated and cylindrical but may be oval. Their legs can be pressed close to the body. Pronotum expanded to form hood-like cover over head. Last three segments of antennae lengthened and expanded.

Adult Biology

Adults are most likely to be found in old woodland with a lot of dead wood or in houses. They are often overlooked for they feign death when disturbed, drawing in their legs and keeping still.

Larvae Characteristics and Biology

Larvae make burrows in wood of buildings and furniture, or in dead trees, leaving piles of fine powder. They can make wood unsafe and reduce it to powder. Adults emerge through small holes. Woodworms (**1**) are larvae of Furniture Beetles.

Common Species

The larvae of **Furniture Beetles** (**2**) and **Death Watch Beetles** (**3**) may infest furniture or structural timbers in old buildings. Death Watch Beetles make a tapping sound as a mating call, supposedly a portent of death. Biscuit and Cigarette Beetles live with their larvae in dried vegetables, spices or tobacco.

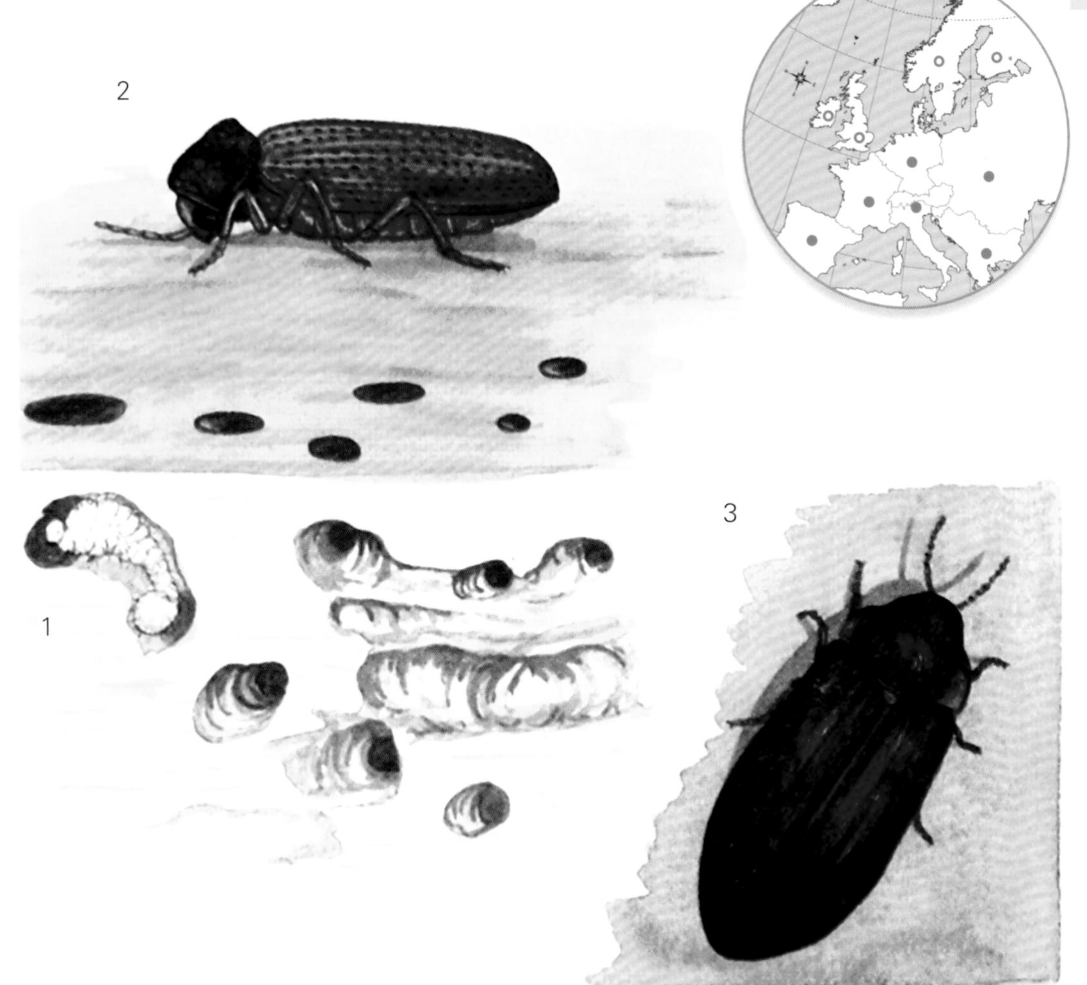
2
1
3

The Death Watch Beetle draws in its legs and keeps completely still, feigning death, when disturbed.

Bark Beetles

About 65 species in Britain

Length: 2–9 mm

Adult Characteristics

Elongated, cylindrical, brown or black beetles with pitted or striated elytra. Antennae short and elbowed, usually with a large rounded club. The elaborate tunnels cut by the adults into wood have distinctive patterns (**1**), depending on species.

Adult Biology

Many Bark Beetles attack trees, making elaborate tunnels just below the bark. Some tunnel into the heartwood; their tunnels are lined with fungus on which they feed.

Larvae Characteristics and Biology

Larvae (**2**) are small, whitish, legless and curled into a C-shape. They are found in tunnels usually cut at right angles to the main tunnels of the adults. They feed in same way as the adults.

Common Species

Adult **Elm Bark Beetles** (**3**) carry Dutch Elm Disease, a fungus disease which has wiped out most elms in Britain and Europe. Ash Bark Beetle attacks diseased or fallen ash trees. Other species infest pines etc. ***Xyleborus dryographus*** burrows into the heartwood (timber) of oaks and chestnuts.

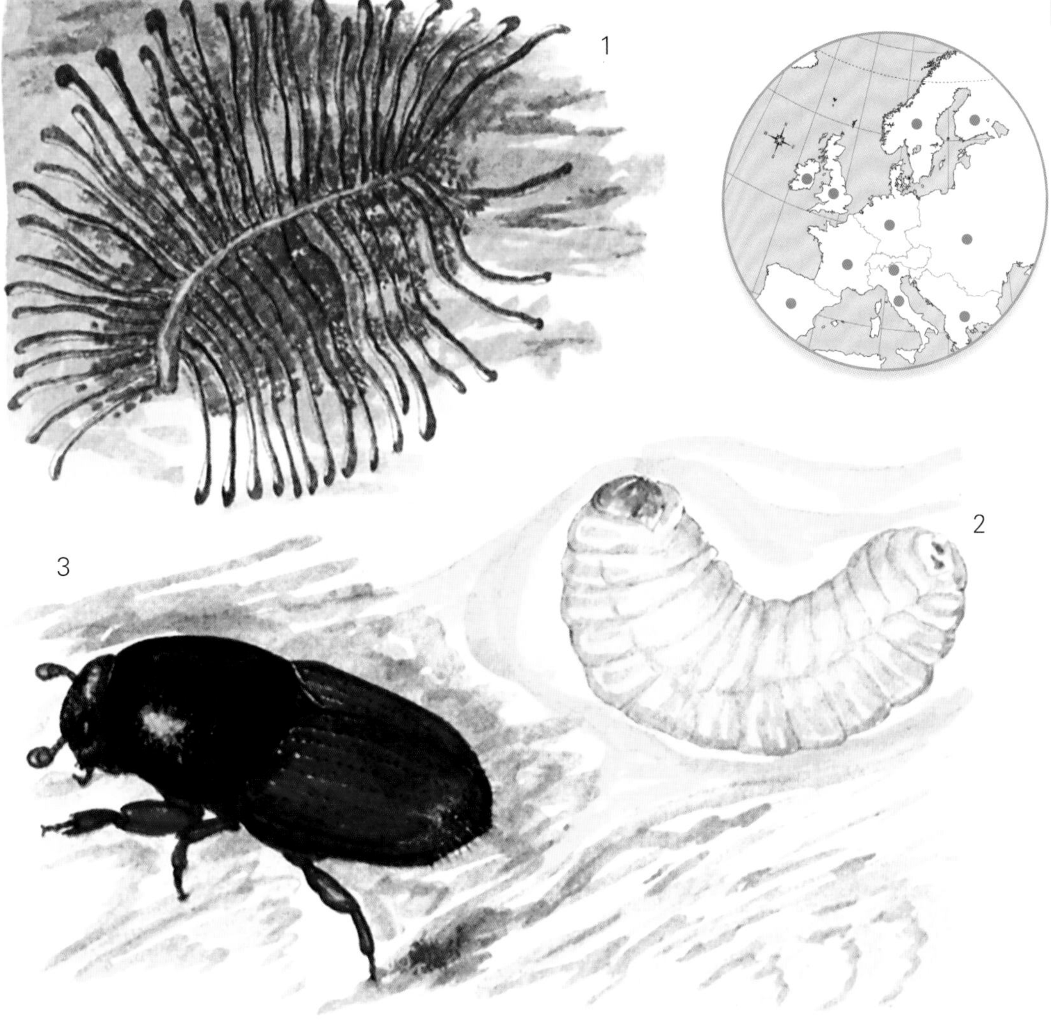
1
2
3

Carpet and Larder Beetles

Length: 1.5–10 mm

About 14 species in Britain

Adult Characteristics

Small, elongated, brown or black beetles, often with pale-grey scales or hairs that are easy to rub off. They may feign death if disturbed, their legs and antennae withdrawn beneath the body. Antennae short and clubbed.

Adult Biology

Adults are scavengers on hide and hair of carrion. Also pests in houses, feeding on stored foods, wool, fur, feathers, meat etc. Some are museum pests, damaging stuffed specimens.

Larvae Characteristics and Biology

Larvae are active, hairy and grub-like; some, clothed in long brown hairs, are called woolly bears (**1**). Most are similar in habits to the adults and can do considerable damage.

Common Species

Carpet Beetles (**2**) may be found on flowers or in windows; their woolly bear larvae (**1**) damage carpets, furs and fabrics; some (museum beetles) attack stuffed mammals and insect collections. **Larder Beetles** (**3**) feed on carrion in the wild but are pests in the home; their larvae feed on dried foods, hides and fabrics.

3

2

1

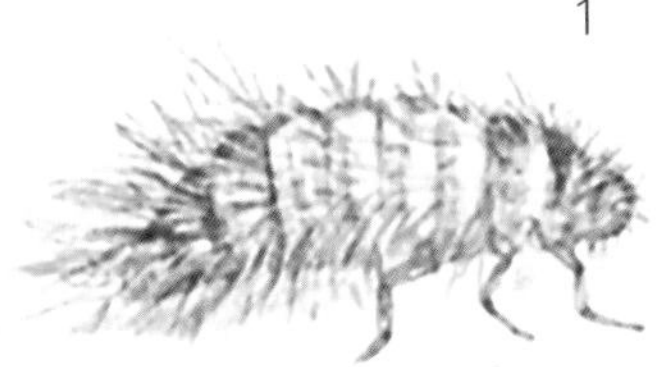

Ladybirds

About 45 species in Britain

Length: 2–9 mm

Adult Characteristics

Round or broadly oval and hemispherical in outline, brightly coloured red and yellow or black and brown, usually with black, white, red or yellow spots. Pronotum partly or completely covers the head. Antennae end in three-segmented clubs.

Adult Biology

Most are predators, feeding on aphids and other pests, found on plants wherever their prey are present. A few feed on plants. Ladybirds may sometimes overwinter in large groups.

Larvae Characteristics and Biology

Larvae (**1**) are variable in form, often camouflaged and spiky, dark in colour or pale and wax-covered. They are mostly predators like the adults, feeding on the same insect pests. Eggs are laid by a female near a colony of the prey species.

Common Species

The familiar red ladybirds have up to 14 spots; they include the **Two-Spot Ladybird** (**2**), which may be red with black spots or black with red spots and the **Seven-Spot Ladybird** (**3**). **Twenty-Two-Spot Ladybird** (**4**) is a small yellow species with many black spots, often found on plants and feeding on moulds.

1
2
3
4

This is a Seven-Spot Ladybird. The number of spots depends on the species – there is a Two-Spot Ladybird and a yellow Twenty-Two-Spot Ladybird.

Longhorn Beetles

About 70 species in Britain

Length: 3–60 mm

Adult Characteristics

Elongated, cylindrical beetles, many large and brightly coloured. Some mimic other insects. Distinctive antennae at least half as long as body and often much longer, up to three times body length. Base of antennae is often partially surrounded by eye.

Adult Biology

Many can be seen by day, near trees or flowers, feeding on pollen. They move and fly swiftly, remaining still if disturbed or squeaking if picked up. Others are nocturnal, hiding by day.

Larvae Characteristics and Biology

Larvae (**1**) are pale and elongated with reduced legs, brown heads and powerful jaws; more bore into wood, making a hole in the bark with sawdust around. Many are pests in forests and orchards, others live in rotting wood and herbaceous plants.

Common Species

A large family of distinctive beetles. Adults, like those of ***Rhagium mordax*** (**2**), can often be seen around trees or flowers in summer. Its larvae live beneath the bark of deciduous trees. The **House Longhorn** (**3**) is a pest whose larvae burrow into telegraph poles and house timbers.

1
2
3

The distinctive antennae of the Longhorn Beetle can be up to three times as long as its body.

Longhorn Beetles

Musk Beetles (**1**) may be seen on flowers or willow trees and emit a pungent, musk-like scent if disturbed. The larvae develop in willows, especially old pollarded ones.

Strangalia maculata (**2**) adults can be seen around flowers in summer but their larvae develop in fallen rotting trees and stumps. Adults may vary in colour from almost all yellow to almost all black. This is one of several similar species, all with distinctive tapering elytra.

Longhorn Beetles

Some longhorn beetles are excellent mimics, like the **Wasp Beetle** (**3**), found usually on timber, in hedgerows and gardens. It is a shy insect that even moves like a wasp, gaining protection from predators like birds who soon learn to avoid wasp stings. Its larvae develop in dead wood, fence posts etc. *Saperda carcharius* (**4**) may be seen on poplars, its presence betrayed by large holes in the leaves where it has been feeding. It has distinctive elytra with dense grey or yellow hairs. The larvae develop in poplar wood.

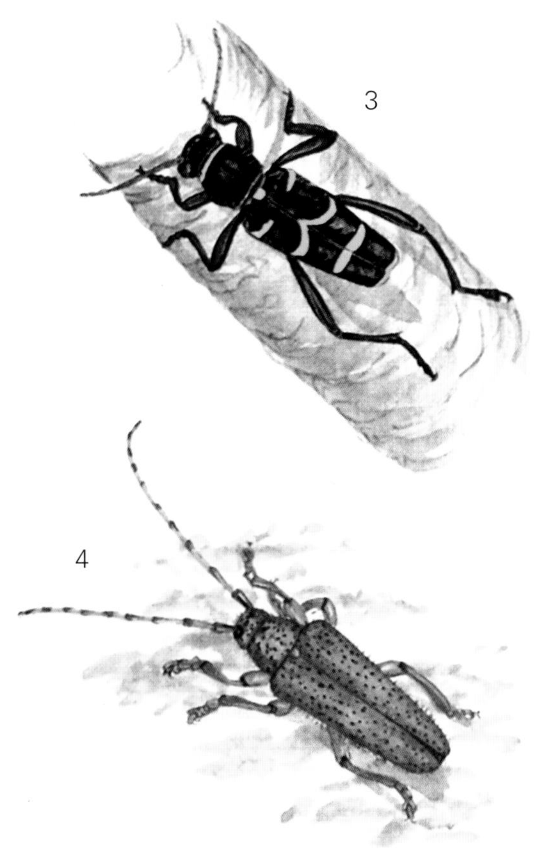

The Wasp Beetle has adopted the appearance and movements of a wasp to deter birds from eating it.

Leaf Beetles

Over 250 species in Britain

Length: 1.5–20 mm

Adult Characteristics

Small, oval and convex in outline. The beetles are often metallic in appearance and attractively marked with various colours. Antennae are less than half the length of the body, thread-like, clubbed or saw-toothed. Eyes not notched.

Adult Biology

Found on all kinds of plants, crops and trees, often together with their larvae. Most adults feed on leaves.

Larvae Characteristics and Biology

Larvae small and slug-like (1), feeding on roots or leaves. Many are serious pests, biting holes in leaves, stripping plants or trees if present in high numbers. Others are tiny and mine tunnels in leaves; tunnels appear as pale lines on the leaves.

Common Species

A large family with many pests, like the **Colorado Beetle** (2), found in central and southern Europe but rarely in Britain; it is a serious pest on potatoes. **Bloody-Nosed Beetle** (3) is one of the largest leaf beetles and is flightless, hiding under stones by day; it exudes a drop of blood from its mouth if disturbed.

1

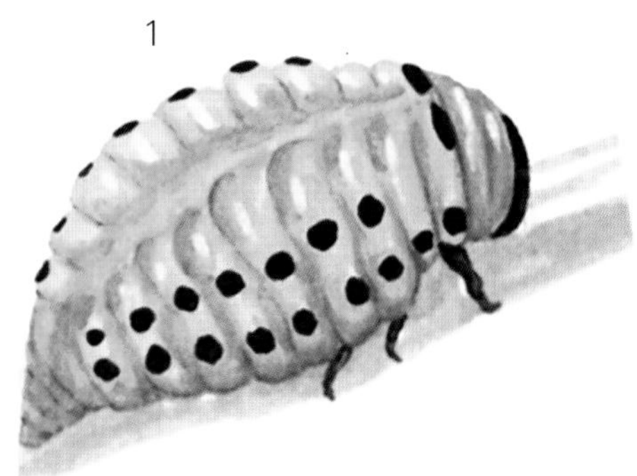

2

3

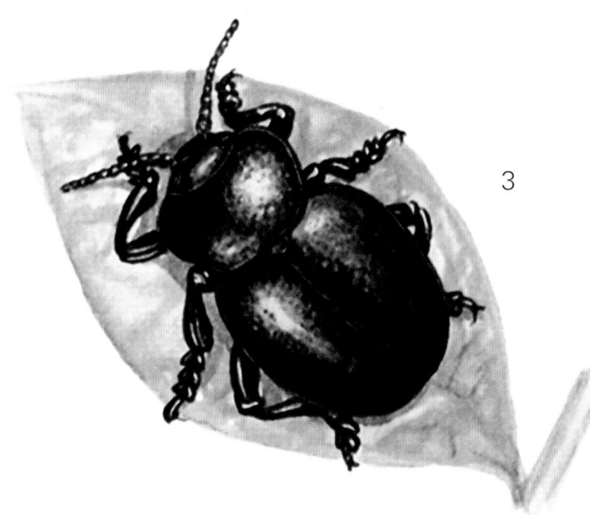

The Bloody-Nosed Beetle will hide under stones by day and exude a drop of blood from its mouth if disturbed.

Leaf Beetles

Many Leaf Beetles are iridescent, like *Cryptocephalus hypochaeridis* (**1**), usually seen on hawkweeds and other yellow-flowered members of the daisy family. The similar but rounder **Chrysolina** species are found on mints, thymes and other members of the mint family. *Lilioceris lillii* (**2**) has become a pest in southern Britain in recent years, invading from Europe and found on lilies. The beetles squeak if handled. Many of these beetles have larvae that camouflage themselves with excrement.

Leaf Beetles

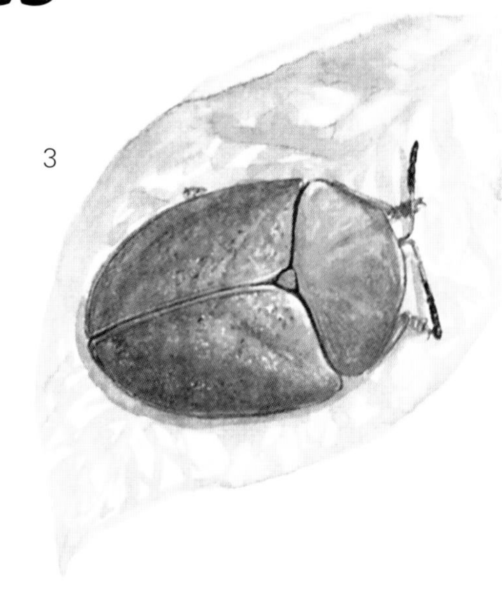

Green Tortoise Beetle (**3**) is one of several almost circular, flattened beetles, looking like small turtles. Their elytra are expanded to cover body and head. Larvae are oval, flattened and spiny, camouflaged with excrement. Adults and larvae bite small holes in plants, often members of mint and daisy families. Flea Beetles are small bluish or black beetles with large hind legs used for jumping. Adults feed on leaves, often on cabbage family members, making tiny holes like shot; larvae feed on roots. Many are pests, like **Turnip Flea** (**4**).

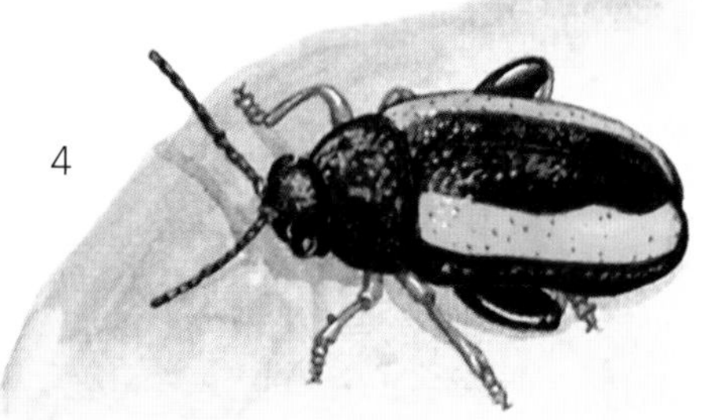

Predaceous Diving Beetles

Length: 2–45 mm

Over 100 species in Britain

Adult Characteristics

Streamlined shiny beetles with flat bodies, usually black or brown (some yellow). Their hind legs are modified for swimming – flattened and fringed with long hairs and moved together. Antennae thread-like. Head sunk partly into thorax.

Adult Biology

Aquatic beetles, found in ponds and lakes; they are fierce carnivores feeding on all kinds of water animals. They come to the surface tail first to obtain air. They also fly well.

Larvae Characteristics and Biology

Larvae (**1**) are even more ferocious predators than adults with large, pointed, hollow mouthparts; they suck the juices from their prey. They are spindle-shaped, brown, with large round heads and well-developed legs.

Common Species

Great Water Beetle (**2**) is one of the largest European beetles; it is found in muddy lakes and ponds throughout Europe and Britain. *Agabus bipustulatus* (**3**) and several similar species are common in ponds and lakes; others are found in streams, rivers and ditches. Many fly to lights at night.

1
2
3

The Great Water Beetle has modified hind legs, so that, like other Diving Beetles, it can swim.

Silver Water Beetles

About 120 species in Britain

Length: 1–50 mm

Adult Characteristics

Black or dark brown, streamlined beetles, silver-coated with a covering of air in aquatic species. Antennae short with terminal clubs, palps long and resembling antennae. These beetles are poor swimmers, with hind limbs only slightly flattened.

Adult Biology

Adults are scavengers, most living in slow-moving or still water, feeding on decaying plants. They hang, head up, at the surface to take in air. Others live in rotting vegetation and damp places.

Larvae Characteristics and Biology

Larvae (1) are often predators, feeding on aquatic animals. They are straight and elongated, flattened with a distinct head and large jaws.

Common Species

Great Silver Beetle (2) has a sharp spine beneath the thorax which can cut unwary fingers; it lives in still weedy waters where the bottom is muddy, mainly in southern Europe and southern Britain. ***Cercyon analis*** (3) lives in compost heaps and decaying plant material throughout Europe.

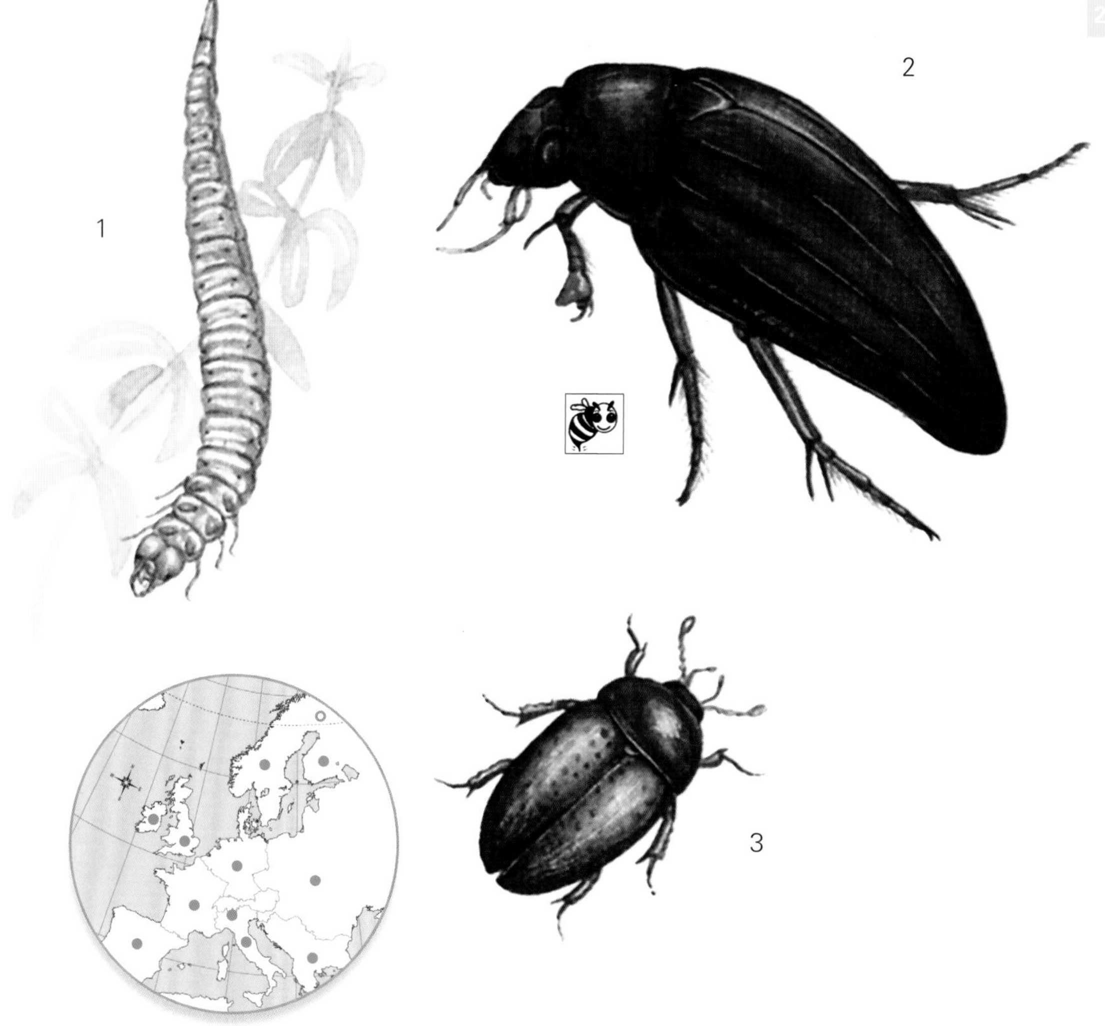
1
2
3

Other Water Beetles

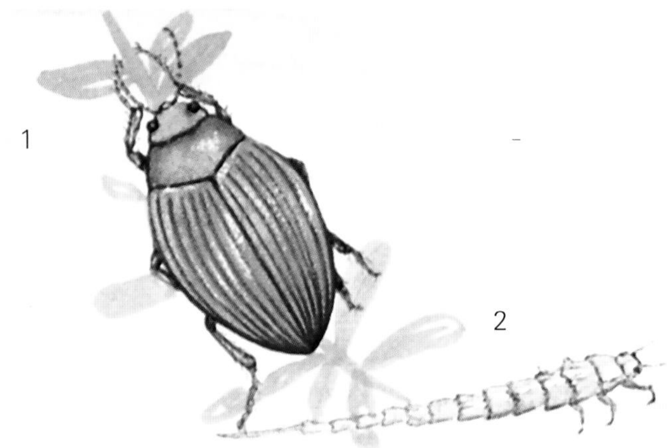

Crawling Water Beetles (1)

About 20 species in Britain. Small, boat-shaped beetles, about 5 mm long, pointed at both ends, yellow or brown with black spots. Found in water with dense vegetation, crawling slowly on the bottom. They feed mainly on green algae and on any insects that they can catch. Larvae (**2**) are slender and their body segments have fleshy lobes with spiny tips. They live in similar habitats to the adults and also feed mainly on algae.

Other Water Beetles

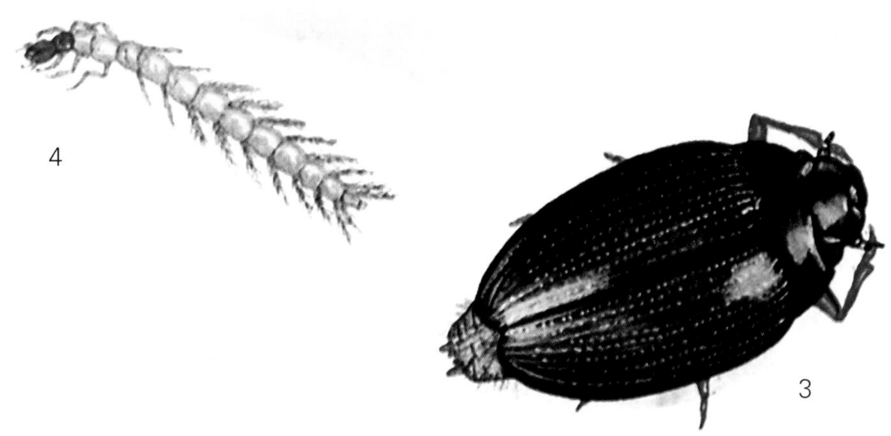

Whirligig Beetles (3)

About 12 species in Britain. Small, black, oval, streamlined beetles, 5–10 mm long, with short antennae. Middle and hind legs short and paddle-like, front legs long and slender. Eyes divided horizontally for seeing in air and water. They swim on ponds, resting on the water surface or on plants, swimming in rapid zig-zags if disturbed. They feed on mosquito larvae and insects trapped in water. Larvae (**4**) long and slender with gills on sides of abdomen; hunt on bottom for insect larvae.

The eyes of Whirligig Beetles are divided horizontally for seeing in air and water while resting on the water surface.

Weevils

Over 500 species in Britain

Length: 2–24 mm

Adult Characteristics

Distinctive, hard-bodied beetles with long snouts. Their antennae are elbowed, with clubs; these antennae arise part way along the snout. Many weevils are covered in fine scales which give them their colour. Several are wingless with fused elytra.

Adult Biology

Found on plants. Adults chew holes in the leaves and may cause extensive damage. They often feign death if disturbed and fall to the ground.

Larvae Characteristics and Biology

Eggs laid in soil or inside seeds, fruits, stems etc. by female who bores a hole with her long snout. Larvae (**1**) short, whitish and curled, with small dark heads and no legs. They live inside seeds, roots, nuts etc. and often do more damage than adults.

Common Species

Vine Weevils (**2**) are pests like many other weevils; their larvae feed on roots of many garden and house plants. Female **Apple Blossom Weevils** (**3**) lay eggs in apple blossom buds which then do not open as the larvae develop inside. Grain Weevils are found with their larvae in granaries, where they do damage.

1
2
3

The female Weevil uses her long snout to bore a hole in seeds, stems or fruit to lay her eggs. Seen here is a Vine Weevil.

Other Beetles

Stag Beetles

Three species in Britain. Small to large, flattened, heavy, brown or black beetles up to 75 mm long. Antennae elbowed with clubs consisting of three or four plates. Males have large jaws, females smaller ones. True **Stag Beetle** (**1**), the males with huge jaws, and **Lesser Stag Beetle** (**2**) both occur in southern and central Europe and in England, in deciduous, often oak woods, on sandy beaches and in towns, hiding by day beneath logs and stumps. Larvae (**3**) are curled into a C-shape, and live in decaying wood.

Other Beetles

Histerid Beetles

About 40 species in Britain. Hard, shiny black beetles, 1–10 mm long, some with red markings. Elytra short, leaving two abdominal segments exposed. Antennae elbowed, with thick button-like clubs. Head, legs and antennae can be drawn beneath the body. Adults and larvae found in rotting vegetation, carrion and dung, preying on other insects. ***Hister 4-maculatus*** (**4**) lives in horse and cow dung. It has four partly joined red spots on a rounded black body. Other species may be all-black.

3

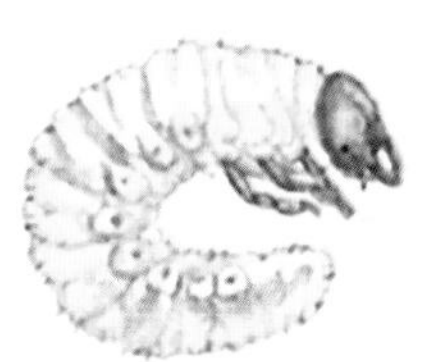

Lesser Stag Beetles can grow up to 75 mm long with large jaws and are found in southern and central Europe and in England.

Other Beetles

Glow-Worms

Two species in Britain. Soft-bodied, elongated beetles with rather soft elytra. Pronotum expanded to cover head. Found in damp grassy places and meadows. **Glow-Worms** (**1**) are winged, larva-like females; in summer evenings they sit on the ground and glow with blue-green light to attract the winged males, the **Fireflies** (**2**). Fireflies are dull brown, flat beetles with parallel sides. Larvae (**3**) are also luminous. Unlike the adults which do not feed, larvae are predators on slugs and snails.

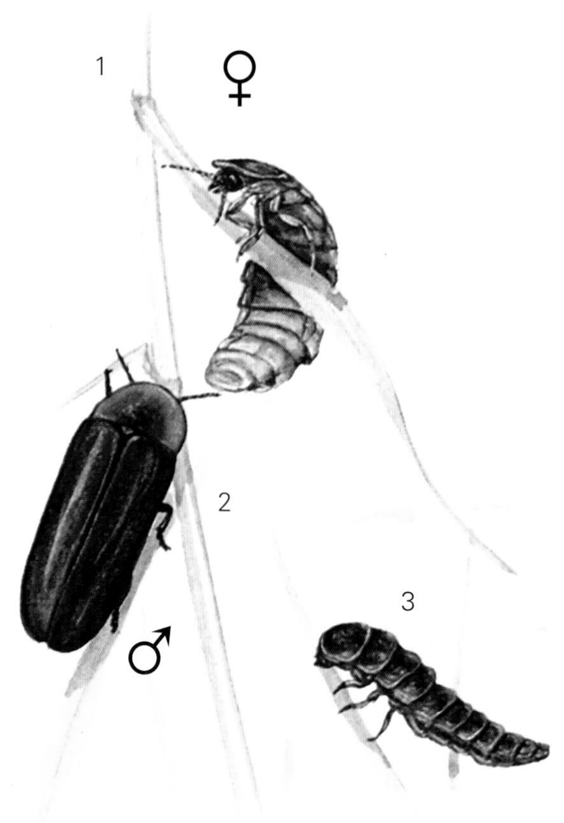

Other Beetles

Jewel Beetles

About 12 species in Britain. Slender, often metallic beetles with pitted or striated elytra. Adults usually seen on flowers. Larvae bore into trees or stems of plants; some are pests. *Agrilus pannonicus* (**4**) is often found around oaks.

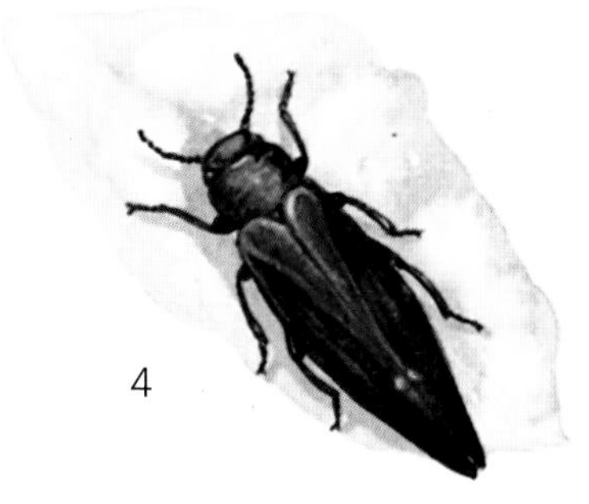
4

5

Checkered Beetles

About 12 species in Britain. Small, bright beetles with long, hairy bodies, soft elytra and clubbed antennae. Most common in woodland, on tree trunks and flowers, like *Thanasimus formicarius* (**5**).

In summer evenings the larva-like female Glow-Worm attracts the male Firefly, shown above.

Other Beetles

Blister Beetles

About 9 species in Britain. Elongated, soft-bodied or leathery beetles, 10–30 mm long, with a narrow neck, broad head and thread-like antennae. Elytra loose. Adults found on leaves and flowers. Larvae parasitic in bees' nests or in grasshopper eggs. **Spanish Fly** (**1**) occurs in warm regions of Europe and southern Britain. Its blood contains the poison cantharidin, once thought to be an aphrodisiac. **Oil Beetles** (**2**) are clumsy, iridescent blue or violet, with short gaping elytra. They exude pungent oily fluid if disturbed.

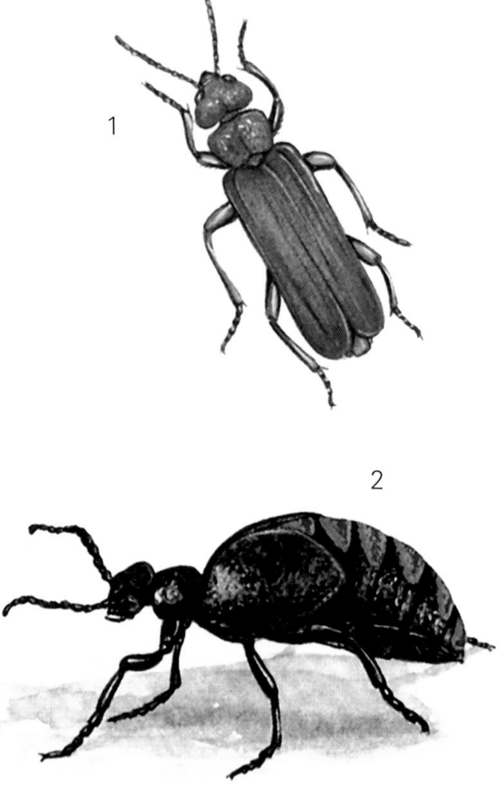

Other Beetles

Sap Beetles

About 90 species in Britain. Small oval, flattened, usually black beetles, often with red or yellow spots. Elytra often short. Antennae have distinct club. Adults and larvae feed on sap, nectar, fermenting fruits and carrion. **Dried Fruit Beetles** (**3**) are pests in fruit stores.

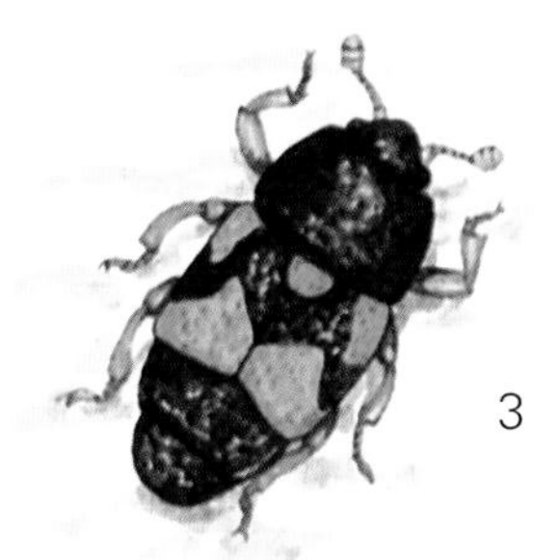
3

Cucujid Beetles

Twenty-three species in Britain. Flat-bodied beetles, many living under bark, others in rotting vegetation. Antennae end in indistinct club. **Saw-Toothed Grain Beetles** (**4**) hunt insect pests in grain stores.

4
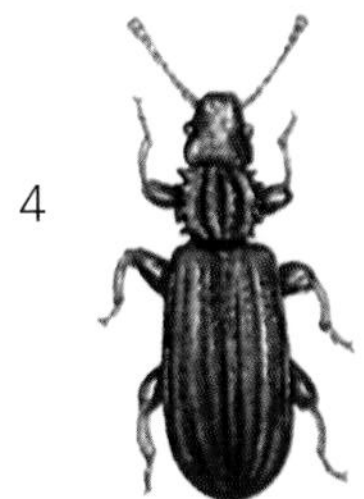

Bugs

Over 500 species in Britain

Length: up to 35 mm

Adult Characteristics

Small to medium-sized insects with two pairs of wings. Fore wings partly horny and coloured, with membranous tips. At rest fore wings are held flat over the back and cover hind wings. Membranous tips of fore wings then overlap.

Adult Biology

Bugs have mouthparts modified for sucking; they suck the sap of plants, or hunt other insects, piercing their prey and sucking out the juices. Some are parasites, sucking blood.

Larvae Characteristics and Biology

Nymphs are usually like small adults but wingless. External wing buds gradually enlarge with each of the five moults. Nymphs have similar lifestyle to adults, with sucking mouthparts which remain the same throughout their life.

Common Species

Many bugs live and feed on plants, including **Stilt Bugs** (**1**), **Fire Bugs** (**2**), Ground, Capsid, Squash and Shield Bugs. Others are predators like **Shore Bugs** (**3**), Ambush Bugs and Damsel Bugs. Bedbugs are blood-sucking parasites. Others are aquatic like **Water Scorpions** (**4**), Water Boatmen and Pond Skaters.

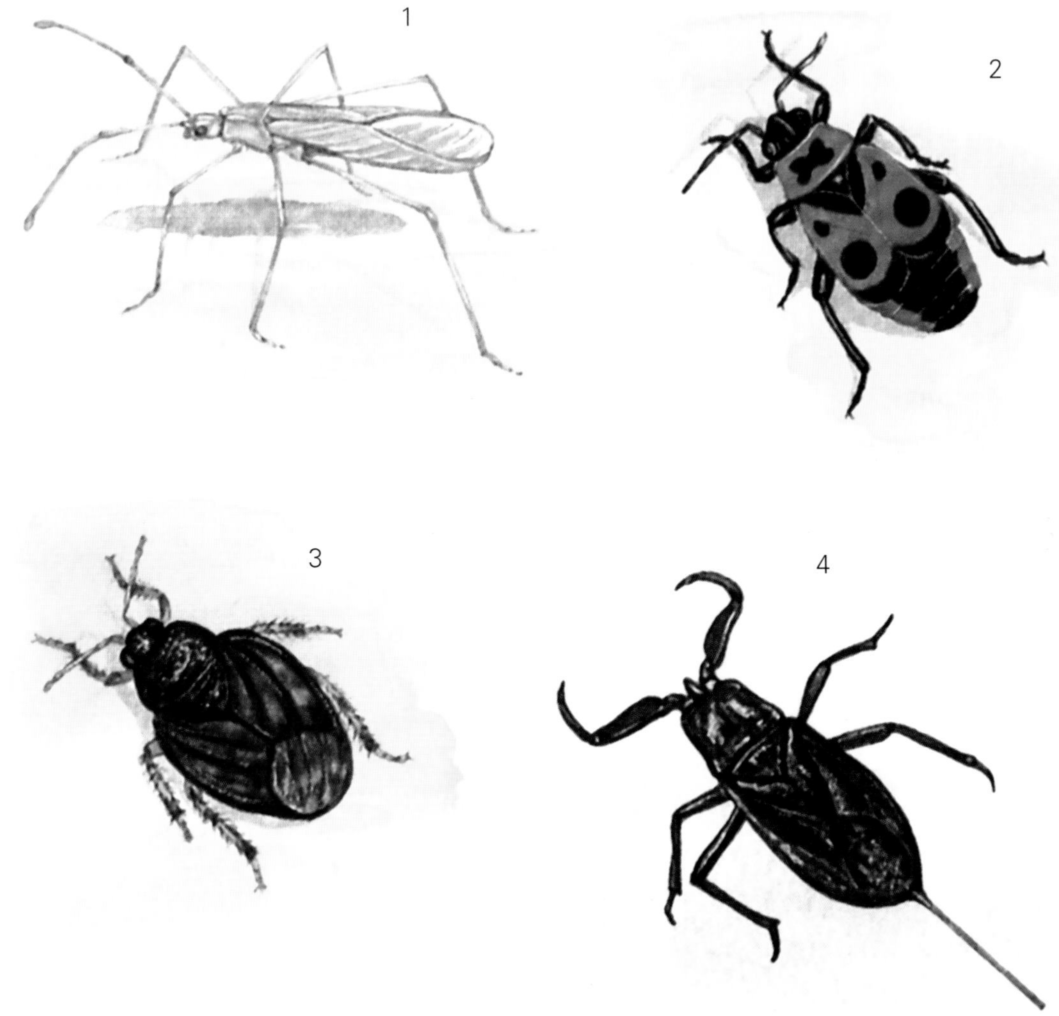
1
2
3
4

The Water Scorpion's name comes from its superficial likeness to the Scorpion. However, it has no stinging tail only an elongated breathing tube.

Shield Bugs

About 40 species in Britain

Length: 3–20 mm

Adult Characteristics

Large, broad-bodied, shield-shaped bugs, many green or brown but some with bright markings. There is a large triangular dorsal shield between the wings. Some have large scent glands on the underside which can exude a foul-smelling liquid.

Adult Biology

Found on all kinds of vegetation, many feeding on plant juices, others hunting other insects. Most often seen in autumn and spring. Some are pests, a few are useful predators on pests.

Larvae Characteristics and Biology

Eggs barrel-shaped and laid in clusters. Young nymphs (**1**) are ladybird-shaped and remain in clusters near eggs. They become flatter and squatter as they moult and tend to scatter. They have no dorsal shield and so look rather different to adults.

Common Species

Parent Bugs (**2**) are found on birch trees; the females stand guard over the eggs until they hatch. **Green Shield Bugs** (**3**) are common on all kinds of plants, especially in hot summers. The large brown Forest Bugs are found in woods and orchards. Tortoise Bugs may damage cereal crops in Europe.

1
3
2

Green Shield Bugs are found on all kinds of plants in summer. Many other species of Shield Bugs eat plants, while others hunt other insects.

Capsid or Plant Bugs

About 200 species in Britain

Length: up to 10 mm

Adult Characteristics

Fragile bugs, with relatively soft, usually elongated or oblong bodies. Fore wings have two distinctive looped veins in the membranous area. Legs and antennae come off easily. Some are brightly coloured but many are camouflaged in green or brown.

Adult Biology

Found on all kinds of vegetation although only a few are pests. The majority feed on plants, often on fruits or seeds. Some are predators on other insects. Many mimic other insects.

Larvae Characteristics and Biology

Nymphs (**1**) similar to adults, lose legs or antennae easily like adults and lead a similar life. Wings buds develop externally, until with the final moult they become wings.

Common Species

The biggest bug family in Britain or Europe. **Tarnished Plant Bugs** (**2**) are found on many herbaceous plants and may cause white spotting on crops, garden plants and weeds. **Black-Kneed Capsids** (**3**) feed on red spider mites; they live on trees, especially apples and lime trees, and are useful in orchards.

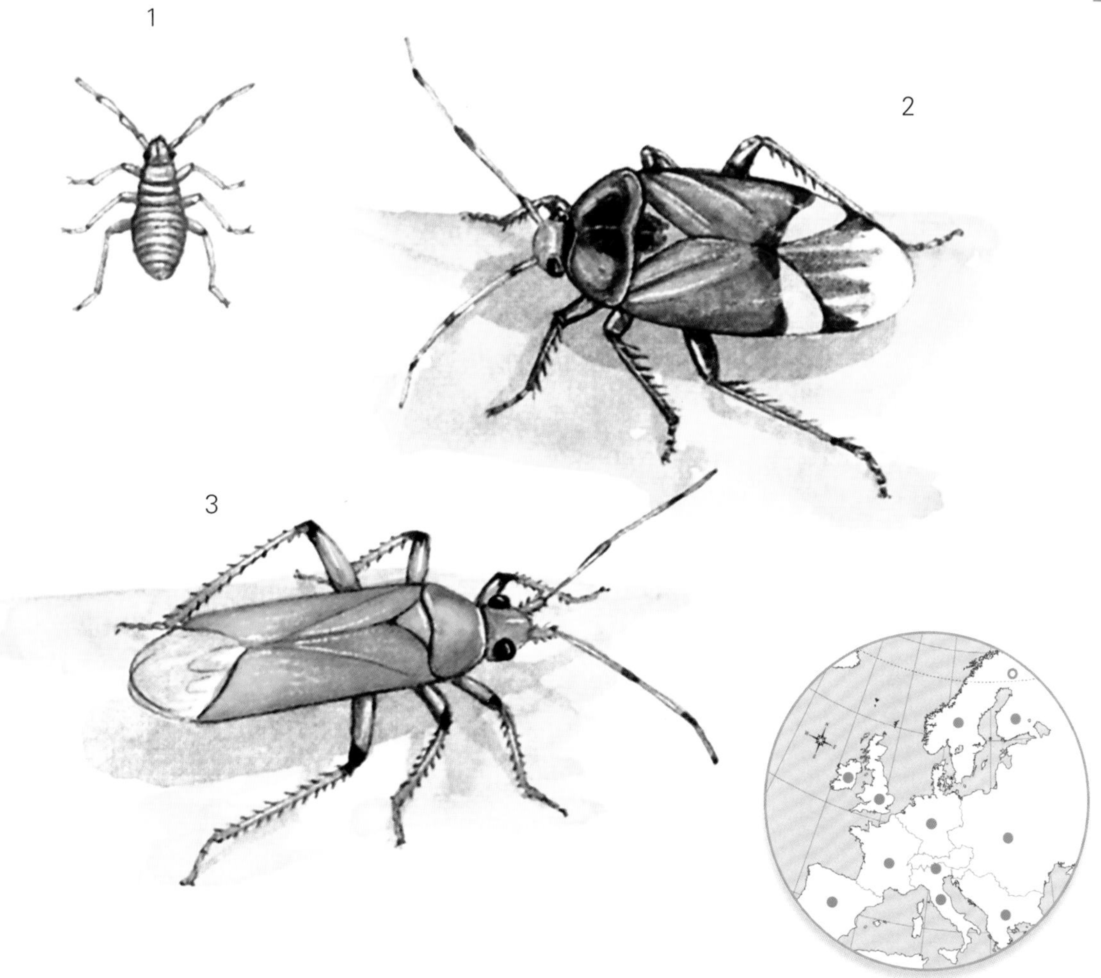
1
2
3

Ground Bugs

About 80 species in Britain

Length: up to 12 mm

Adult Characteristics

Elongated or oval, hard-bodied bugs, usually dark brown or black in colour, many with red markings. They have only five distinct veins in the membranous area of each fore wing and have no looped veins in the fore wings.

Adult Biology

Many feed on the seeds of grasses and other plants or suck plant juices; some prey on other insects. They are found in meadows and heaths, in fields and hedgerows, in leaf litter, on trees etc.

Larvae Characteristics and Biology

Nymphs (**1**) are similar to adults but wingless. Their wing buds enlarge gradually with each moult. They lead similar lives to the adults and are found in the same places.

Common Species

European Chinch Bugs (**2**) swarm on seed heads of grasses and reeds, sometimes on cereal crops; some individuals are winged while others are wingless. **Nettle Ground Bugs** (**3**) are common on and around stinging nettles.

1
2
3

Flower Bugs and Bedbugs

Length: 2–8 mm

About 30 species in Britain

Adult Characteristics

Small, sombrely coloured, brown or black bugs, usually with horizontally flattened bodies and faces. Some species lack wings. Winged species have fore wings clearly divided into five distinct areas, separated by sutures.

Adult Biology

The winged flower bugs live on plants, preying on aphids, thrips, mites and other insects. Bedbugs suck the blood of birds and mammals, living in nests and lairs of their hosts.

Larvae Characteristics and Biology

Nymphs live in similar places and have similar lifestyles to adults. In winged species their wingbuds enlarge with each moult until fully formed in adults.

Common Species

Common Flower Bug (1) stalks its insect prey in summer, hibernates beneath bark in winter. The related Debris Bug lives in compost heaps, haystacks or granaries. **Bedbugs** (**2**) and their nymphs (**3**) live in houses, hiding in crevices or bedding by day, coming out at night to suck blood from sleeping people.

1
2
3

Pond Skaters

15 species in Britain

Length: 10–12 mm

Adult Characteristics

Bugs with long bodies and long middle and hind legs, which rest on the water making little dimples on the surface. The body is covered in thick velvety, waterproof hair which stops the insects from becoming trapped in the water.

Adult Biology

Semi-aquatic insects which 'skate' on the water of ponds, lakes and streams; some live on the sea. They feed on insects trapped on the water, holding them with their fore legs.

Larvae Characteristics and Biology

Nymphs similar to adults and with similar lifestyle, but smaller. Wings buds develop externally, enlarging with each moult until with the final moult they become wings.

Common Species

Common Pond Skaters (**1**) are found on almost any still waters. The similar **Water Measurer** (**2**) has a very thin elongated body and very long legs; it is often wingless and walks slowly over water weeds or on the water of ponds. The smaller, stouter water crickets live on streams and ponds, running on the water.

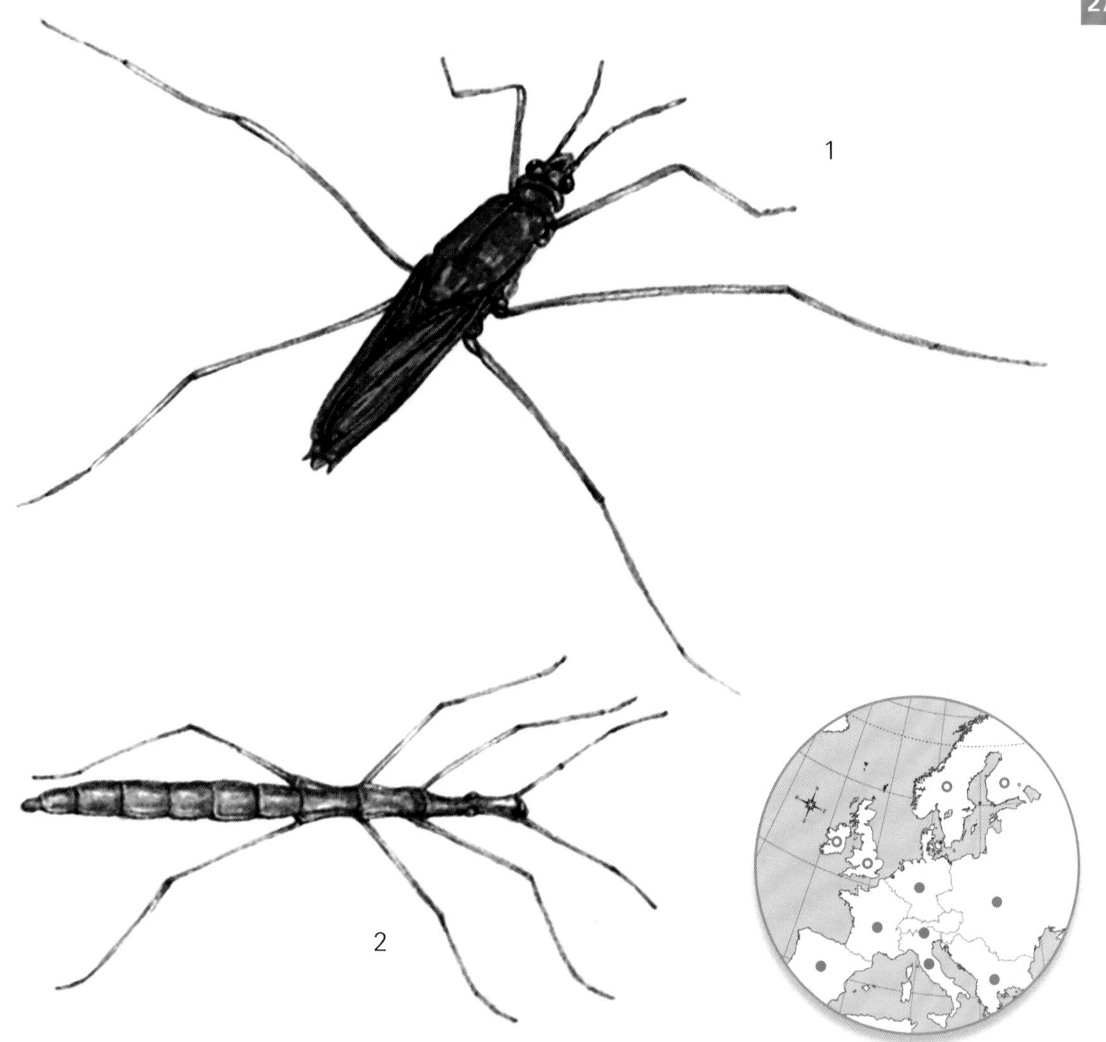
1
2

The body of the Pond Skater is covered with thick, velvet, waterproof hairs, which prevent it becoming trapped under the water.

Water Bugs

Backswimmers (1)

About 4 species in Britain.

Backswimmers look like boats with a pair of oars; they swim on their backs and have large flattened hind legs which they use like oars. They may bite if handled. Found in ponds and lakes, often resting at the surface, head down with abdomen projecting into air. They are predators, feeding on fish, tadpoles and other creatures. Nymphs similar to adults and with similar lifestyle, but smaller and with developing, not functional wings. Adults grow about 15 mm long; they are good fliers.

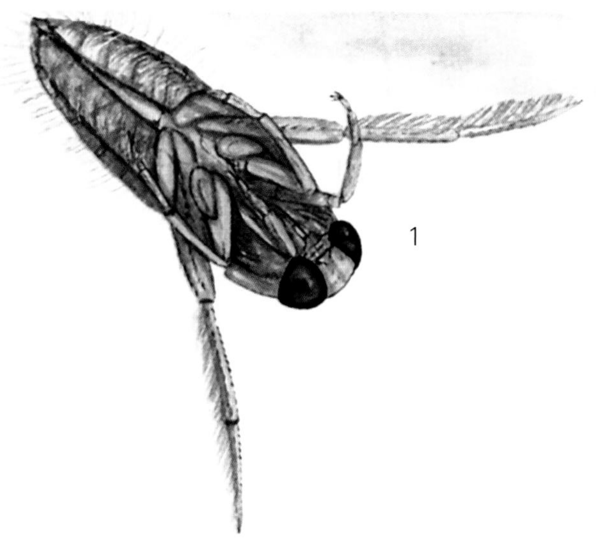

Water Bugs

Water Boatmen (2)

About 30 species in Britain. Water Boatmen resemble Backswimmers but use both hind and middle legs as oars and swim the right way up. Found in ponds and lakes. They often stay close to the bottom, clinging to rocks or weeds, feeding on plant debris and algae. Nymphs similar to adults and with similar lifestyle, but smaller, with developing not functional wings. Adults grow about 12 mm long and fly well.

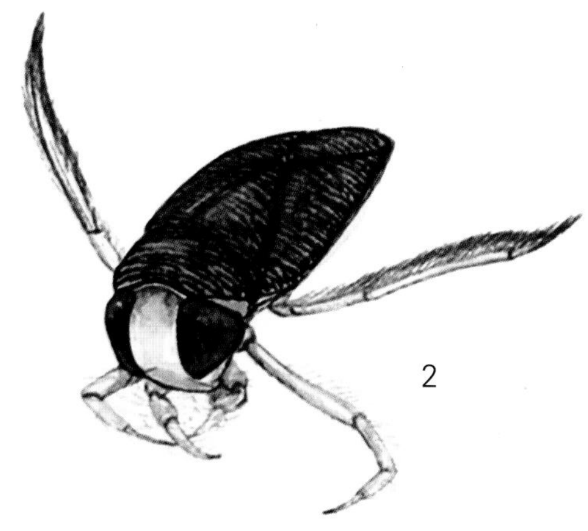

Backswimmers are found abdomen-side-up in ponds and lakes where they rest near the surface.

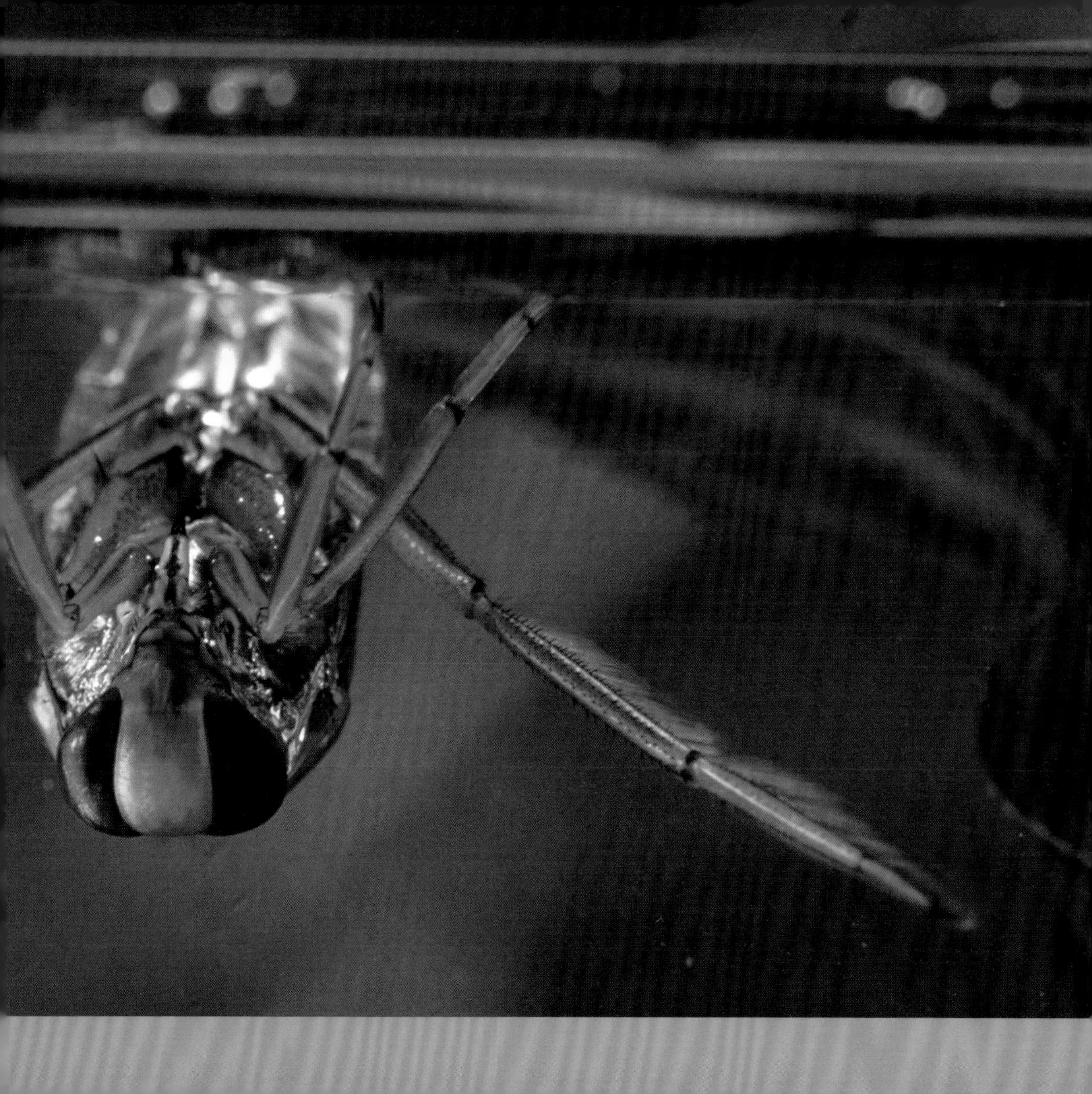

Predatory Bugs

Assassin Bugs

Six species in Britain. Robust or elongated, usually brown bugs, 5–20 mm long, with long legs; front legs may be spiny and used for catching prey. Abdomen often broader than wings. Fierce predators, hunting insects and often mimicking their prey; they may bite or make a noise if handled. **Heath Assassin Bug** (**1**) is a short-winged insect found on heaths and sand dunes. The fully winged Fly Bug is attracted to lights at night; it lives around houses, hunting flies and bedbugs.

1

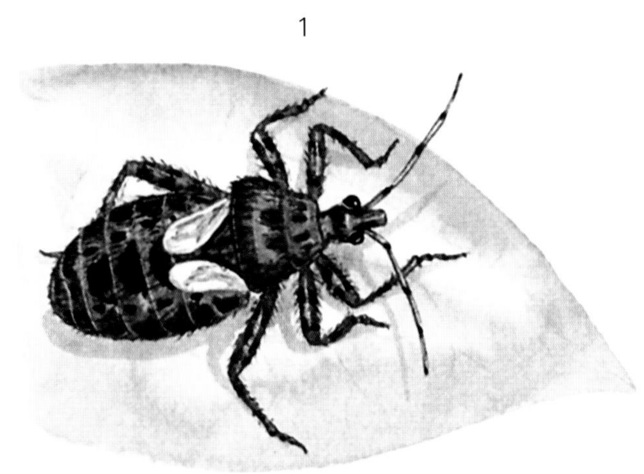

Predatory Bugs

Damsel Bugs

About 12 species in Britain. Small brown predatory bugs like assassin bugs, but more slender, up to 10 mm long, with relatively long legs. Adults and nymphs most often found among grasses or low vegetation, hunting insects like aphids and caterpillars. Prey are seized in fore legs and stabbed with the beak, then their juices are sucked out. Adults fly well. **Common Damsel Bug** (**2**) is typical, found in almost any grassy area. Marsh Damsel Bug is similar but has short wings and lives in damp grassy places.

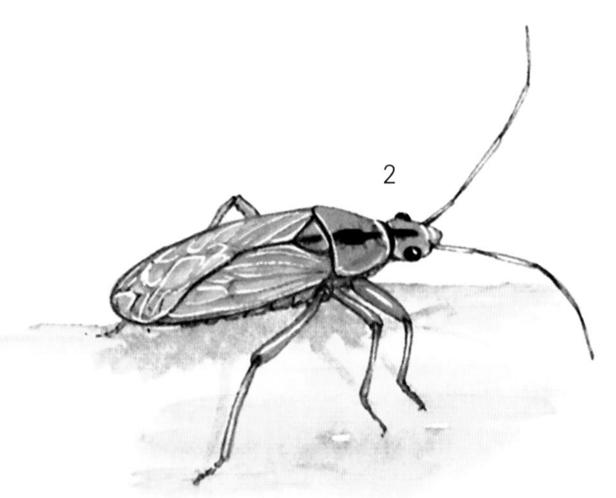

Other Bugs

Squash Bugs

Twenty-one species in Britain. Large, often dull-brown, more or less elongated bugs, up to 15 mm long, often with an expanded abdomen and broad dorsal shield. Some have spines or tubercles on head and thorax. Antennae stout and strong, especially in young nymphs. Head narrow, eyes large. May exude a foul-smelling liquid if disturbed. These bugs are found on plants, often feeding on fruits and seeds. Nymphs found in same places as adults; they often have lateral spines and long antennae. *Coreus marginatus* (**1**) is found on docks and sorrels in summer.

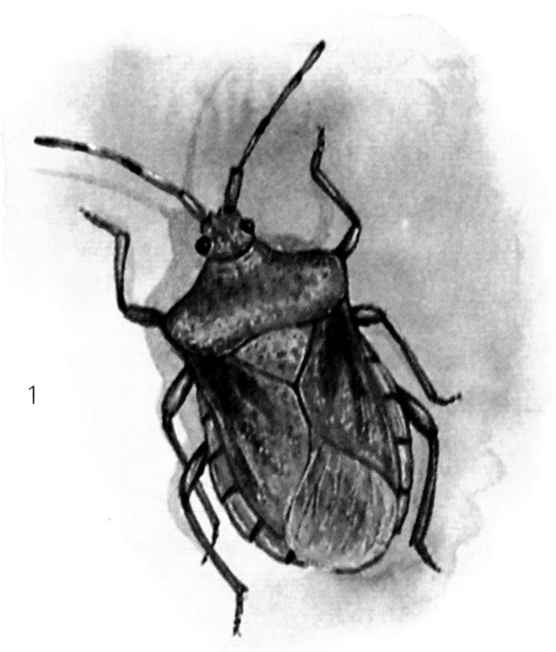

Other Bugs

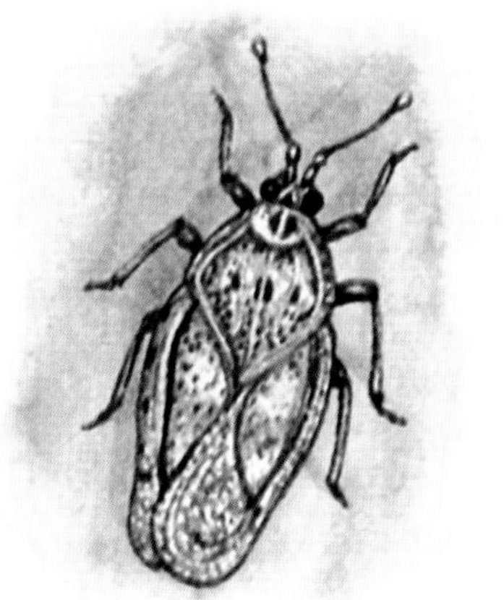

Rhopalid Bugs

Ten species in Britain. Similar to Squash Bugs, but usually red and/or black in colour. Fore wings often membranous. Found on plants, many feeding on seeds and fruits. ***Rhopalus subrufus*** (**2**) is found in woods and hedgerows.

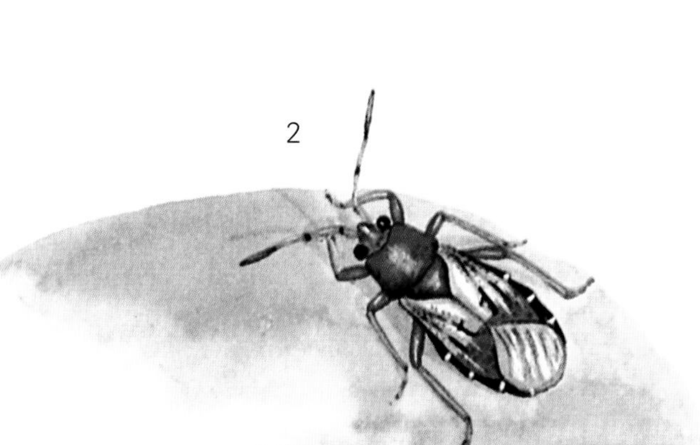

Lace Bugs

About 20 species in Britain. Small, flattened bugs, up to 5 mm long. Often greyish and covered in wax. Thorax and fore wings look like lace. Adults and nymphs found beneath leaves or in mosses. Nymphs often spiny and darker than adults. **Spear Thistle Lace Bug** (**3**) lives on thistles.

Homopteran Bugs

Over 1100 species in Britain

Length: mostly 1–10 mm; to 35 mm

Adult Characteristics

Mostly small insects with two pairs of similar horny or membranous wings (i.e. homopterous) or wingless. Wings often held in a roof-like position over the body when at rest. All have sucking mouthparts which originate far back beneath the head.

Adult Biology

All feed on plants, sucking out their juices with their sucking mouthparts. They may be found on any part of a plant, from roots to leaves, stems, flowers and fruits.

Larvae Characteristics and Biology

Nymphs often similar in form to adults but wingless. Life cycle may be normal with nymphs developing through several moults into adults, or may involve alteration of winged and wingless forms, as in aphids.

Common Species

Many are pests on economically important plants. They include cicadas, aphids, whiteflies, hoppers, scale insects and mealybugs. Illustrated on this page are **Mussel Scale** on apple bark (**1**); **Long-Tailed Mealybug**, a greenhouse pest (**2**); **Apple Psyllid** (**3**), another apple pest; and **Horned Treehopper** (**4**).

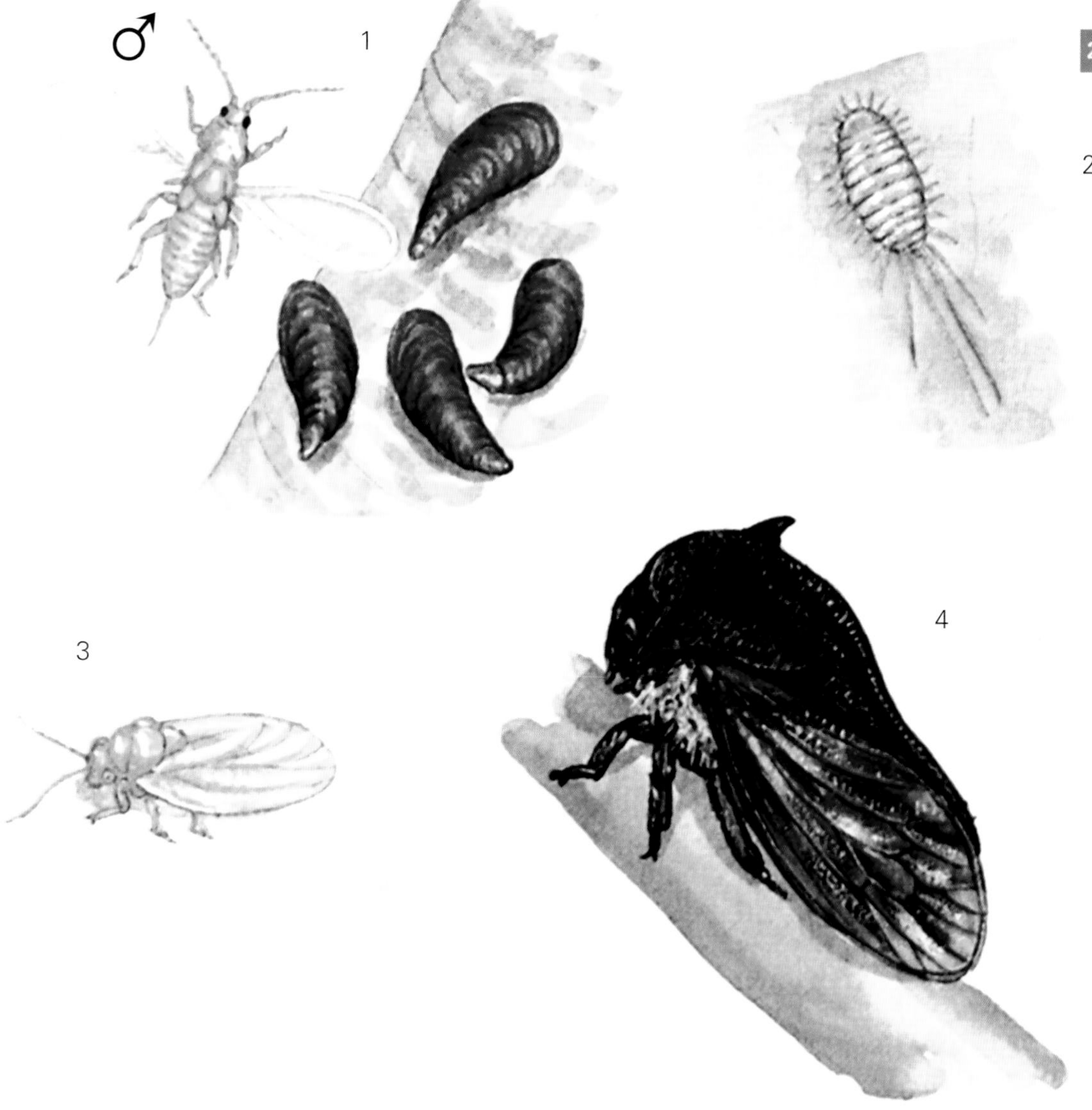
♂
1
2
3
4

Whiteflies

About 20 species in Britain

Length: 1–2 mm

Adult Characteristics

Adults tiny, covered with white powder and with transparent, whitish or spotted wings. They look like tiny moths, with two pairs of proportionally large wings. Hind wings slightly larger than fore wings.

Adult Biology

Mostly tropical insects. One is a greenhouse and house plant pest.

Larvae Characteristics and Biology

Nymphs (**1**) are tiny oval creatures, attached to the undersides of the leaves by minute threads. Final nymph resembles a pupa. Nymphs and adults suck sap from leaves and cover them with a sticky honeydew on which moulds grow, turning them grey.

Common Species

Several species are found in Europe and Britain. Some are pests, like Cabbage Whitefly which causes considerable damage to cabbages and other brassicas. **Greenhouse Whitefly** (**2**) attacks a variety of greenhouse and house plants, particularly tomatoes, cucumbers and fuchsias. Nymphs resemble scale insects.

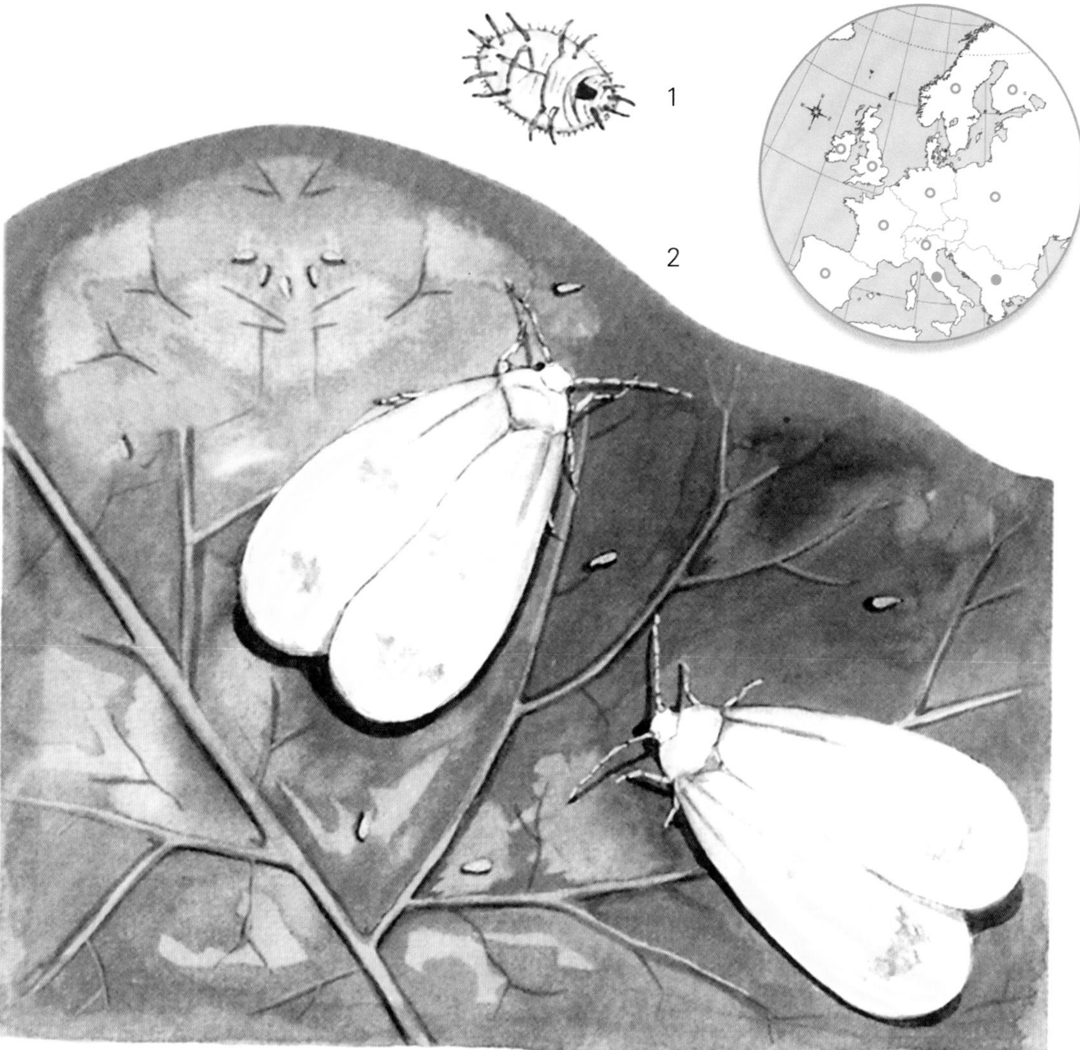
1
2

Aphids

Over 500 species in Britain

Length: up to 5 mm

Adult Characteristics

Small, soft-bodied, pear-shaped insects, usually green, brown or red, winged or wingless. Wings held vertically above body. Pair of cornicles (wax-producing organs) are present at the rear of the abdomen. Aphids have a pointed sucking 'beak'.

Adult Biology

Pests of cultivated and wild plants; often present in large numbers, causing leaf distortion and weakening of plants from which they suck sap. Often tended by ants for their honeydew.

Larvae Characteristics and Biology

Wingless females hatch from eggs in spring on host plant, and produce wingless, then winged females. These fly to different plants and multiply again. In autumn winged forms fly to original plant to produce males and females. Eggs laid then overwinter.

Common Species

Aphids attack trees like pines, oaks, willows and apples; also many wild plants; and crops like wheat, broad beans and cabbages. Common garden pests include **Greenfly**, pests on roses (nymph (**1**), wingless form (**2**) and winged form (**3**)) and **Blackfly** (**4**), (pests on beans and other plants).

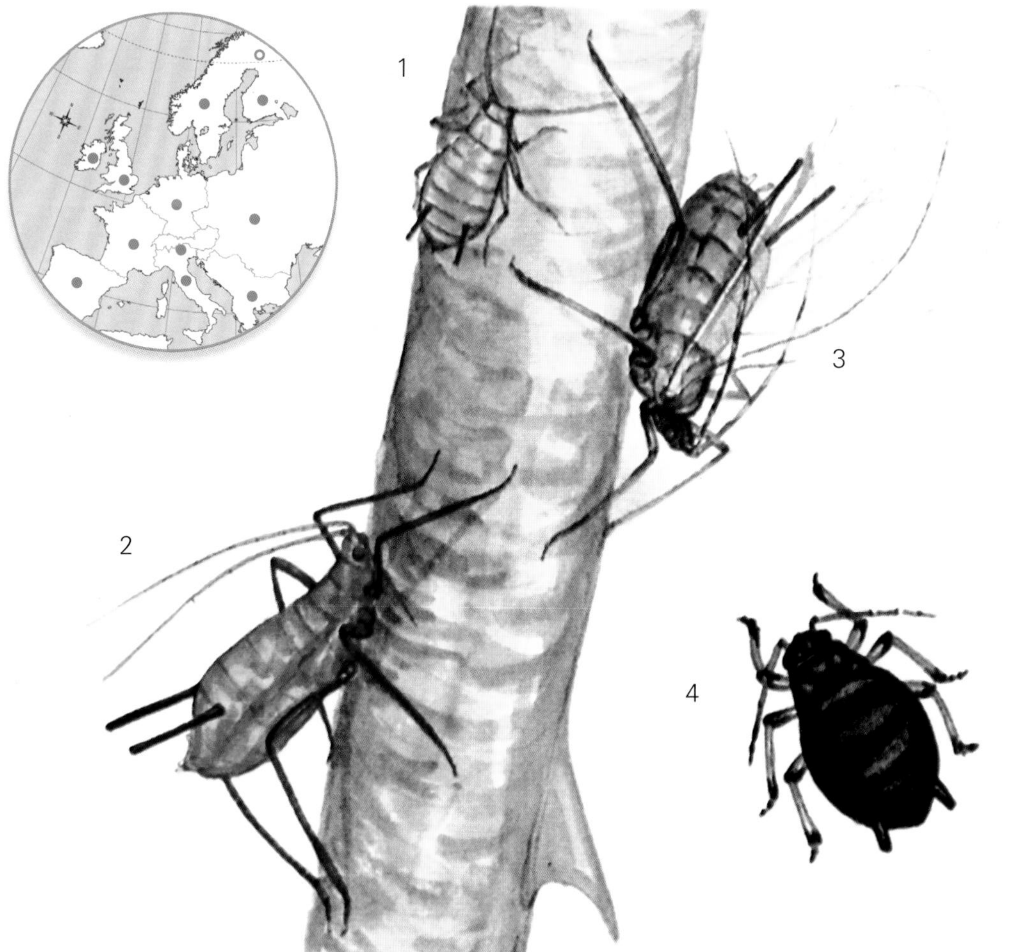
1
2
3
4

Froghoppers

10 species in Britain

Length: 5–10 mm

Adult Characteristics

Oval or elongated insects, usually brown but some brightly coloured. Fore wings are horny and legs have few spines. The pronotum is large but does not extend over the abdomen. Two tiny antennae arise on the front of the head between the eyes.

Adult Biology

Adults jump like tiny frogs. They (and their nymphs) occur in meadows, gardens and woods. They suck sap from plants, especially on the new growth, and may weaken them.

Larvae Characteristics and Biology

Nymphs of many species (**1**) live in masses of bubbly froth (cuckoo-spit) which protects them from drying up and from predators. They produce the froth by secreting 'spit' from the anus; it trickles over the body and mixes with air.

Common Species

The familiar cuckoo-spit of gardens and hedgerows comes from **Common Froghoppers**; nymphs are green and adults (**2**) dull brown. Adult **Red-And-Black Froghoppers** (**3**) are larger. They live mainly in woodland where the nymphs develop underground, surrounded by solidified froth and feeding on roots.

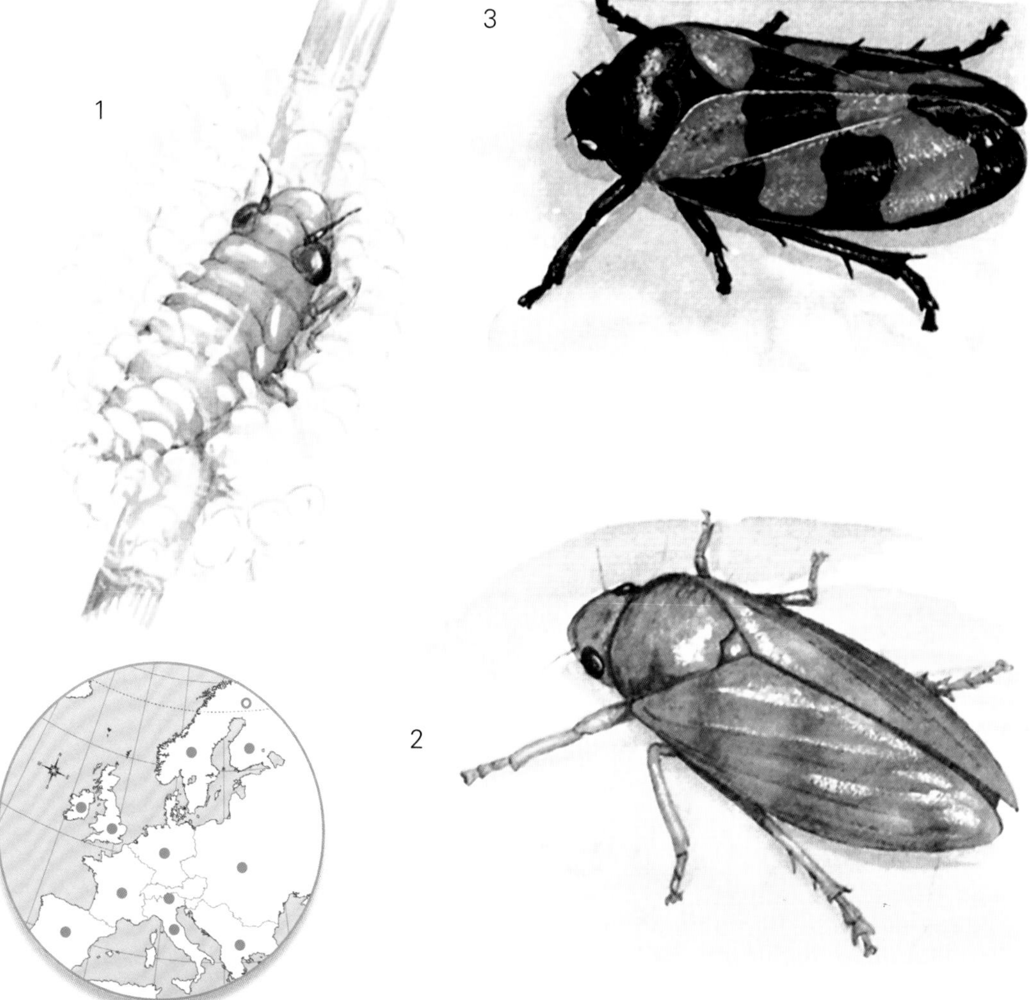
3
1
2

Cicadas and Leafhoppers

Cicadas

Large, blackish insects with two pairs of transparent, membranous wings, fore wings twice as long as hind wings. Adults sit in shrubs and trees, males singing to attract females. Nymphs (**1**) develop in the ground, sucking juices from plant roots. After a period of years they emerge, climb into trees and moult to become adults. Several species occur in Europe, one in Britain. *Cicadetta Montana* (**2**) (wingspan about 50 mm) is rare, found in the New Forest.

Cicadas and Leafhoppers

Leafhoppers

About 250 species in Britain. Small, jumping insects like long froghoppers, up to 10 mm long, many green or brightly coloured. Antennae arise on head between the eyes. Common on trees, shrubs and herbaceous plants, in meadows, orchards, gardens and woods. They suck sap from plants, leaving a pale blotch around the injury. A few are pests. Many exude honeydew. **Green Leafhopper** (**3**) lives on grasses in damp meadows. *Eupteryx aurata* (**4**) lives on nettles and members of the mint family; can be a pest on potatoes.

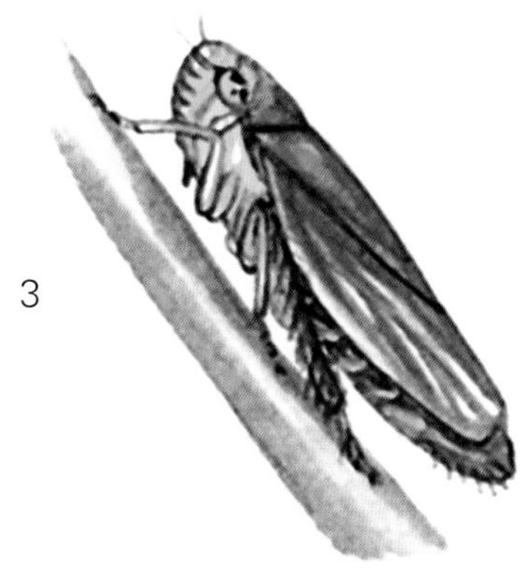

3

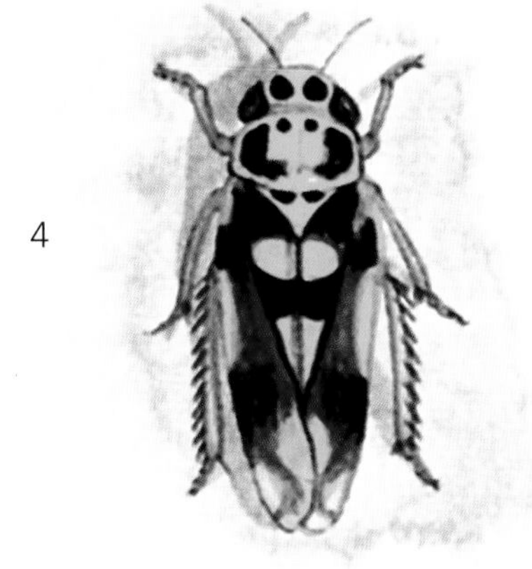

4

Grasshoppers and Crickets

Length: mostly 5–40 mm

30 species in Britain

Adult Characteristics

Large insects with long back legs and two pairs of wings. Fore wings long, narrow and leathery, protecting membranous hind wings which are folded beneath fore wings when at rest. Head flat-sided with large biting mouthparts. Pronotum large.

Adult Biology

Grasshoppers feed mostly on plants, bush-crickets on insects. Many jump and glide rather than fly. Males often have characteristic 'songs', used in territorial and courtship behaviour.

Larvae Characteristics and Biology

Adults of many species lay eggs in summer and autumn which then overwinter and hatch in spring. Nymphs are similar to adults but wingless; wing buds develop gradually, enlarging with each moult. Nymphs are found in similar places to adults.

Common Species

Includes bush-crickets, crickets and grasshoppers, a few of them pests like **Locusts** (**1**). **Mole Crickets** (**2**) burrow into soft soil; they are widespread in Europe, rare in southern England. **Greenhouse Camel-Crickets** (**3**) are invaders from Africa found in greenhouses. **Groundhoppers** (**4**) are like silent grasshoppers.

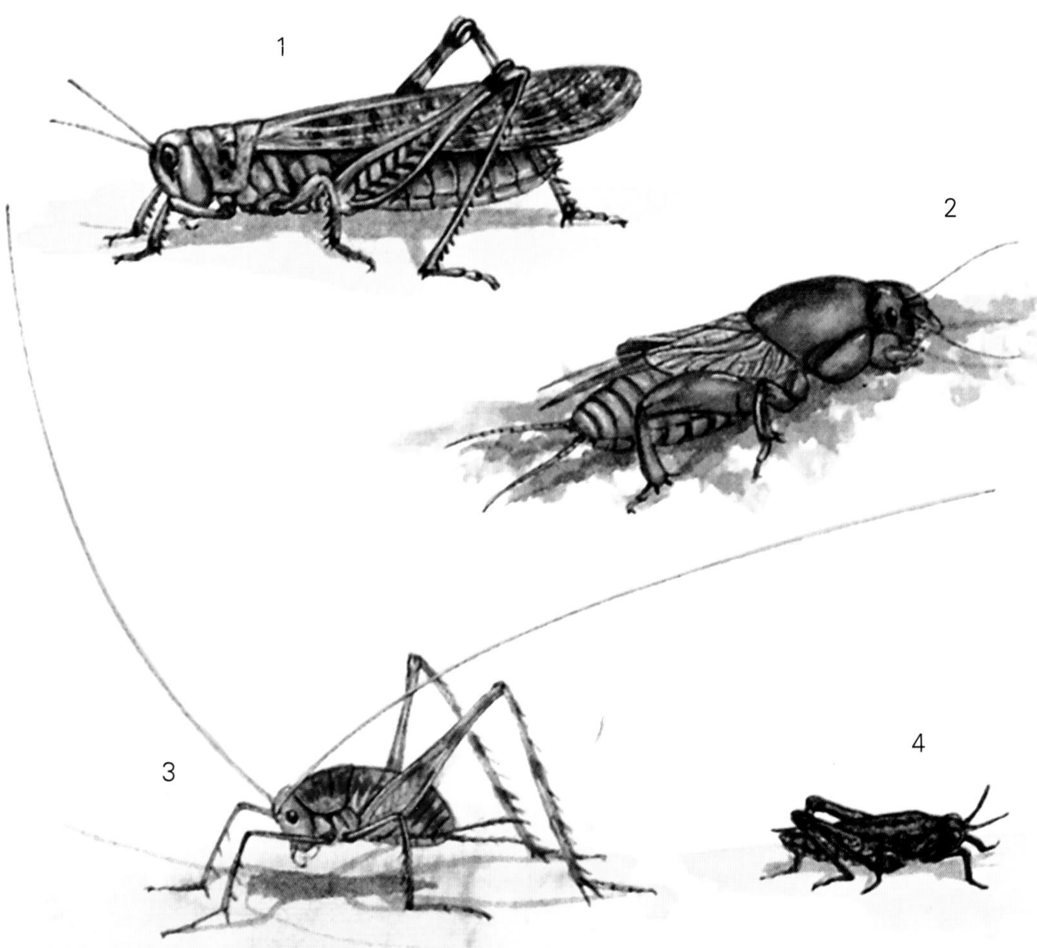
1
2
3
4

Short-Horned Grasshoppers

Length: mostly 12–30 mm

11 species in Britain

Adult Characteristics

Antennae short and stout, less than half the length of head and thorax combined. Males make a low buzzing sound by rubbing rough surface of the femur of the hind leg on hardened veins on fore wing. Ear drums present on each side of abdomen.

Adult Biology

Active by day; males 'sing' loudest in hot sun. Most common in grasslands and mixed woods where they feed on plants, often grasses. Many jump with their powerful hind legs; others fly.

Larvae Characteristics and Biology

Most short-horned grasshoppers have one brood, laying eggs in summer and overwintering as eggs. Nymphs live in similar habitats to adults; they are like small adults with developing wing buds instead of wings.

Common Species

Some are widespread, familiar roadside and grassland species, like the Common Field Grasshoppers (1) and Common Green Grasshoppers (2). Some can be destructive pests, like the Locusts which occur in southern Europe, usually as solitary insects but sometimes in swarms; they can grow up to 60 mm.

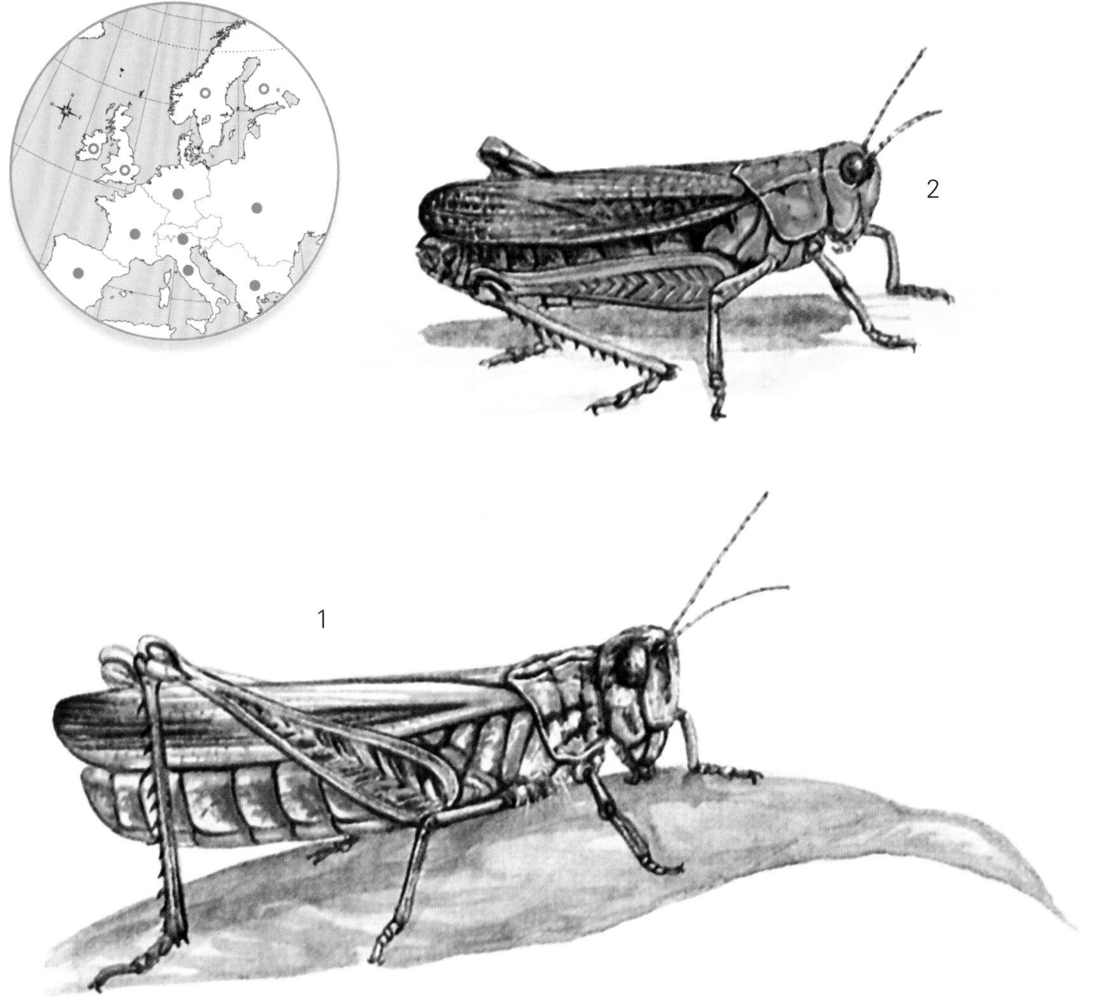
2
1

The Common Green Grasshopper is usually found alone, but is noticed by his song.

Bush-Crickets

10 species in Britain

Length: mostly 20–40 mm

Adult Characteristics

Antennae long and slender, often longer than body. Males make sounds by rubbing fore wings one against the other; right wing has a rough patch which is rubbed against vein on left. Ear drums present on fore wings. Female has sword-like ovipositor.

Adult Biology

Many sing at dusk and by night, a few by day, each species with its own song. Adults occur in wet grassland, marshes, hedgerows and woodland edges. They feed on plants and other insects.

Larvae Characteristics and Biology

Nymphs appear in early summer and live in similar habitats to the adults, but may remain close to the ground or live in dense vegetation. They are like small adults with developing wing buds instead of wings.

Common Species

Many species are green, others brown. One of the largest is the **Great Green Bush-Cricket** (**1**), found in gardens, cultivated land and roadsides in lowland Europe and southern Britain, hiding in vegetation like the **Speckled Bush-Cricket** (**2**). This widespread species is found in gardens and woods.

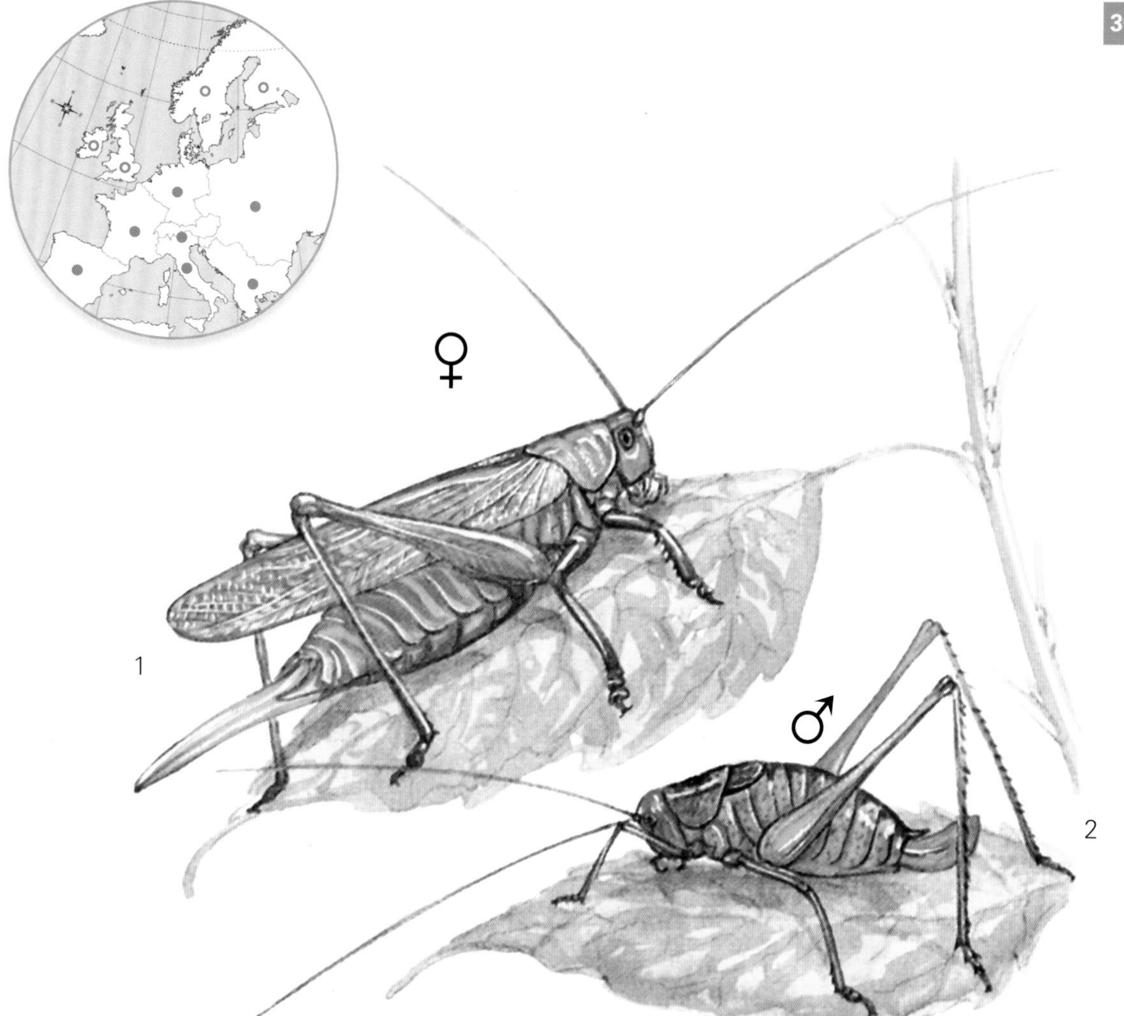

♀
1
♂
2

The Great Green Bush-Cricket hides in vegetation in the gardens, cultivated land and roadsides of lowland Europe and southern Britain.

Crickets

4 species in Britain

Length: 7–25 mm

Adult Characteristics

Brown or black, flattened insects, their long antennae up to half the length of the body. There are long conspicuous tail filaments at the end of the abdomen. Males produce sound by rubbing fore wings together. Females have long cylindrical ovipositors.

Adult Biology

Found on the ground or in burrows, many flightless. Males sing on summer nights, chirping or trilling. Adults feed on plants, stored foods or other insects.

Larvae Characteristics and Biology

Nymphs overwinter, developing from eggs laid the previous summer. Older nymphs live on the ground or in burrows. They are similar to adults and feed on similar foods. Wing buds develop gradually, enlarging with each moult.

Common Species

House Crickets (1) may be found in old buildings or around rubbish tips in summer. **Field Crickets** (2) live in dry fields, heaths and sunny banks in Europe, and in a few places in southern Britain. Pale yellow-brown Tree Crickets are common on bushes and trees in Europe but absent from Britain.

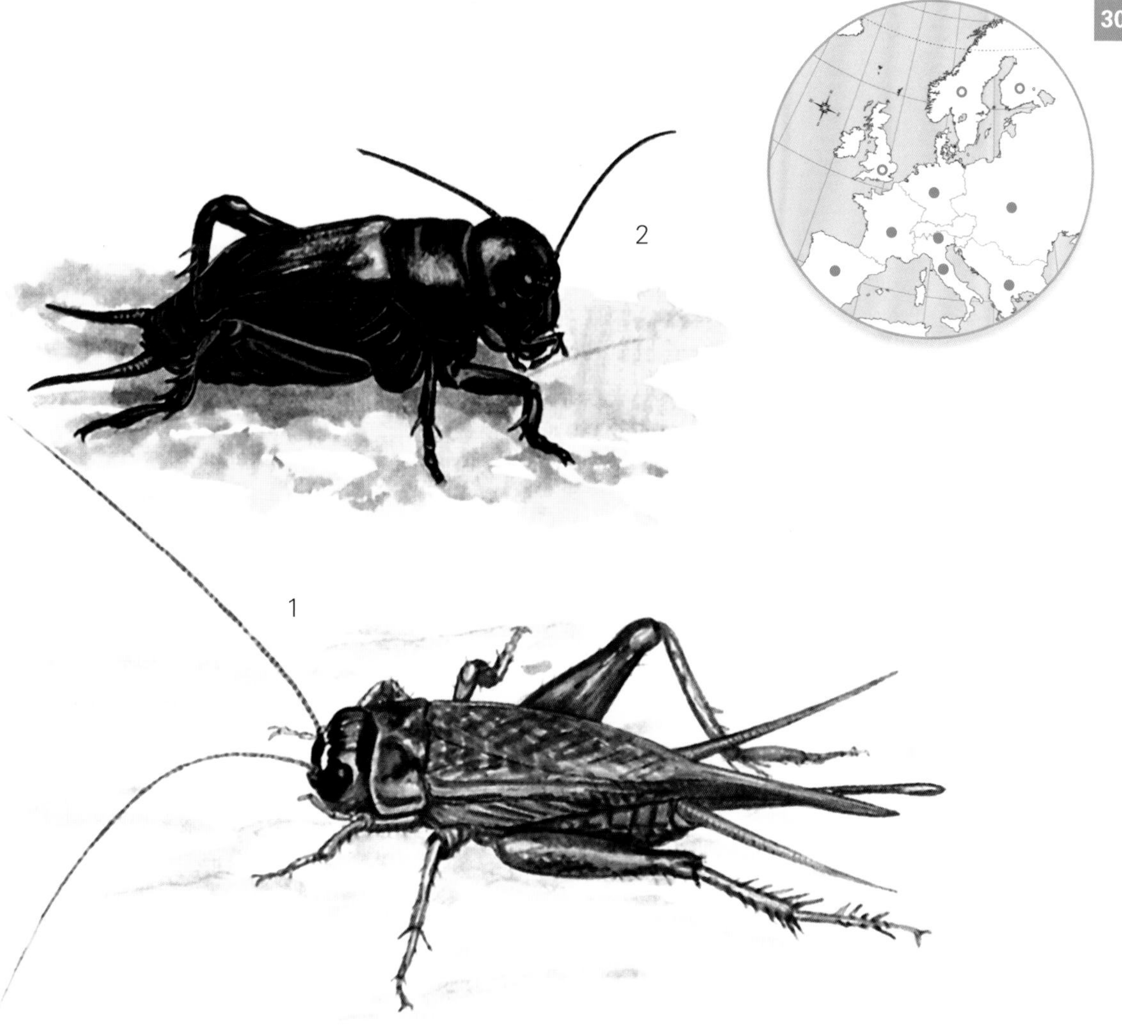
2
1

Field Crickets are rare in southern Britain and are more easily spotted in the day fields on the Continent.

Cockroaches

10 species in Britain

Length: 7–35 mm

Adult Characteristics

Flattened, oval, reddish-brown insects. Head hidden by pronotum. Antennae long and slender. Fore wings thickened and covering the folded, membranous hind wings when they are not in use; but wings may be absent.

Adult Biology

Many are fast-moving scavengers in houses, restaurants and food stores, hiding by day to emerge by night and feed. They contaminate what they do not eat with their musty odour.

Larvae Characteristics and Biology

Female carries around and then lays eggs in leathery egg capsule in dark crevice. Nymphs are like miniature adults but wingless. Wing buds, if present, enlarge gradually with each moult; nymphs have similar lifestyle to adults.

Common Species

The cosmopolitan American Cockroach (1) has large wings and it flies; it is common in warm buildings. Also cosmopolitan, the Oriental Cockroach (2), often known as a 'Blackbeetle' is dark reddish-brown; males have shortened wings but females are wingless. It is common in houses and kitchens.

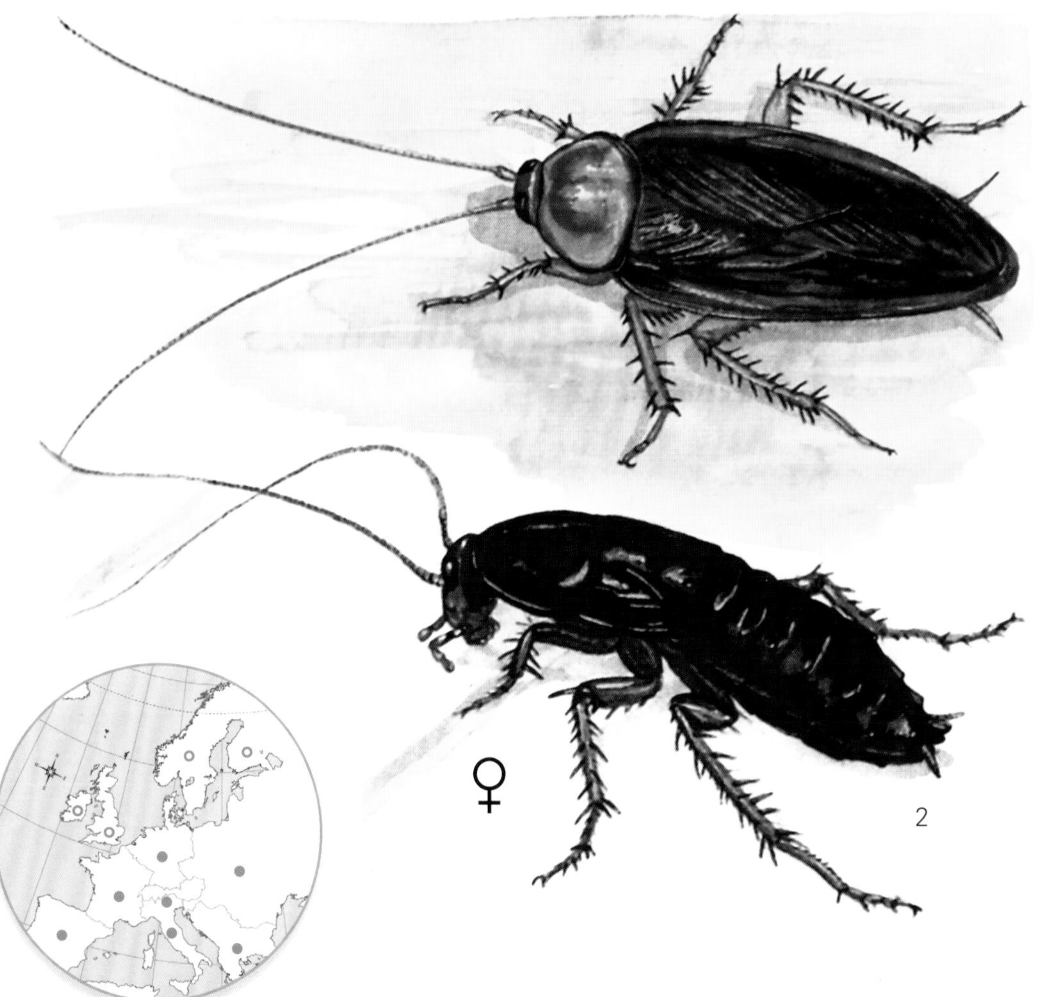
1
♀
2

Lacewings

About 60 species in Britain

Length: 5–25 mm; wingspan to 50 mm

Adult Characteristics

Soft-bodied, green or brown insects with two pairs of membranous wings, usually held in a roof-like position over the body. Wings have many net-like veins. Antennae long. Lacewings have no tail filaments.

Adult Biology

Mainly nocturnal. Found in grassland, gardens and other open areas, also in woods and dense vegetation, also in houses. They feed on aphids, scale insects, mealybugs and mites.

Larvae Characteristics and Biology

Green Lacewings lay eggs on leaves or twigs, each on a long stalk; larvae (**1**) are flattened and elongated; some decorate themselves with debris. Brown Lacewing eggs are not stalked but the larvae are similar. All feed on insects like adults.

Common Species

Giant Lacewing is a large brown insect with spotted wings and a wingspan of up to 50 mm, found near streams and rivers. **Green Lacewings** (**2**) are smaller (12–25 mm wingspan), and are green with green wings and golden eyes. **Brown Lacewings** (**3**) are smaller still (5–12 mm wingspan) with brown wings and eyes.

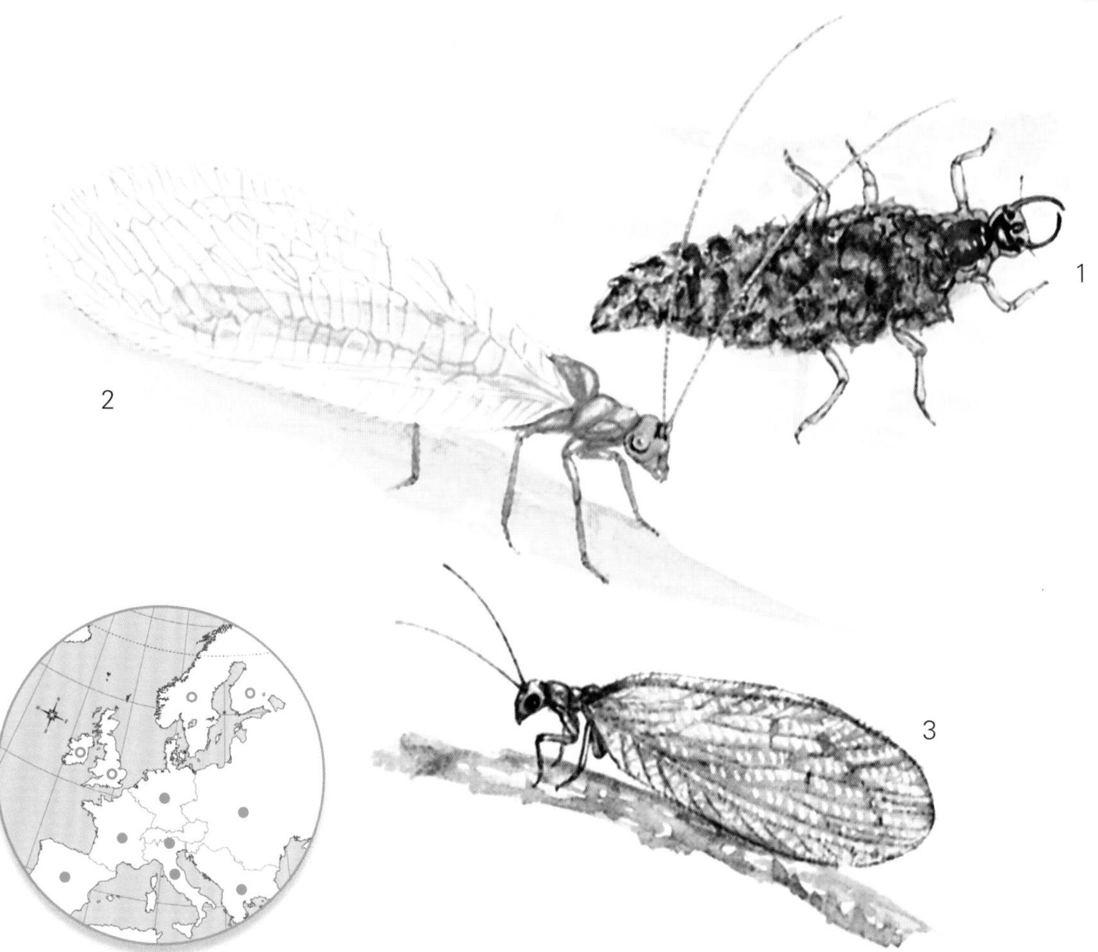
1
2
3

The larvae of Green Lacewings are predatory and are used in agriculture to rid crops of aphid pests.

Caddis or Sedge Flies

Length: up to 25 mm

About 190 species in Britain

Adult Characteristics

Elongated, cylindrical, soft-bodied insects, brownish in colour with no tail filaments. They have two pairs of large, hairy, membranous wings, held in a roof-like position at rest. Wings have few cross-veins. Antennae as long as wings or longer.

Adult Biology

Adults (**1**) are poor fliers with erratic flight, mainly flying at dusk and they may be attracted to lights. Hide by day in crevices or vegetation near water and feed but little.

Larvae Characteristics and Biology

Larvae are like caterpillars, with hard heads and biting jaws, three legs on the thorax and two strong hooks at the tip of the abdomen. They live in water, many in cases of wood pieces, sand grains or shell fragments; others spin nets or live free.

Common Species

Casemaker caddis larvae, like **Great Red Sedge** larvae (**2**), make cases out of plant fragments; larvae of **Silver Sedges** (**3**) and Brown Silverhorns make cases out of sand grains. Both live in lakes and rivers. Free-living caddis larvae, like those of **Sandflies** (**4**), live among stones in fast-flowing streams.

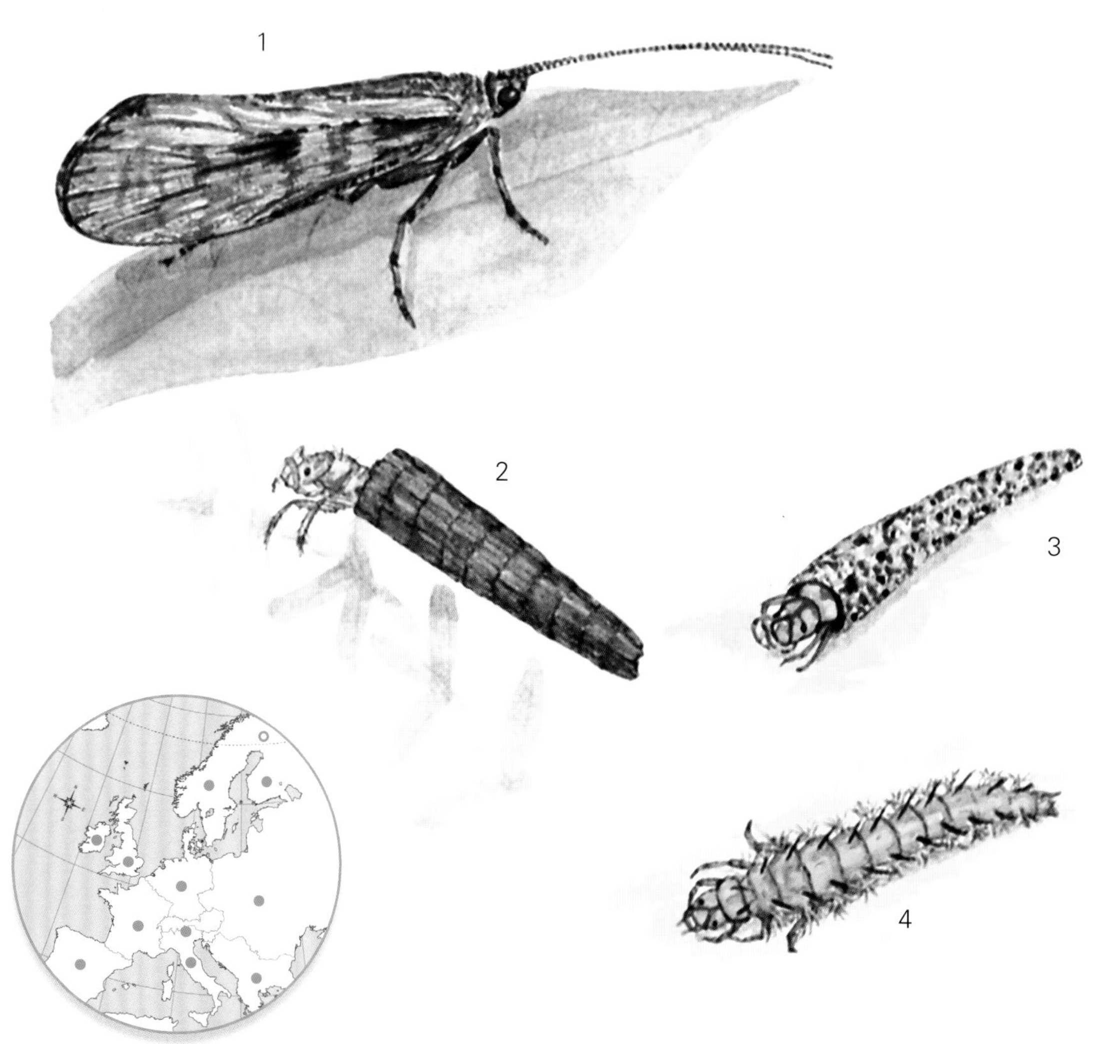
1
2
3
4

Dragonflies

25 species in Britain

Length: 30–85 mm; wingspan 45–110 mm

Adult Characteristics

Stout-bodied insects with two pairs of large membranous wings. Wings have complex veins and cross veins. When at rest they hold their wings horizontally to the sides. The head is large and freely movable with large eyes and biting mouthparts.

Adult Biology

These are large predaceous insects which pursue their prey, other insects like mosquitoes, on the wing. They fly by day, most often over and near water.

Larvae Characteristics and Biology

The large nymphs (**1**) live in water of ponds and streams, feeding on other water insects, catching them with a 'mask', a large hinged lower lip which can be swung out at lightning speed to grasp the prey.

Common Species

Hawker Dragonflies are the largest dragonflies, with long bodies; they may fly long distances, often patrolling a definite route, like the **Emperor Dragonfly** (**2**), found in Europe and southern Britain. Darter Dragonflies, like **Common Sympetrum** (**3**) have shorter bodies; they often sit on shrubs, darting out at prey.

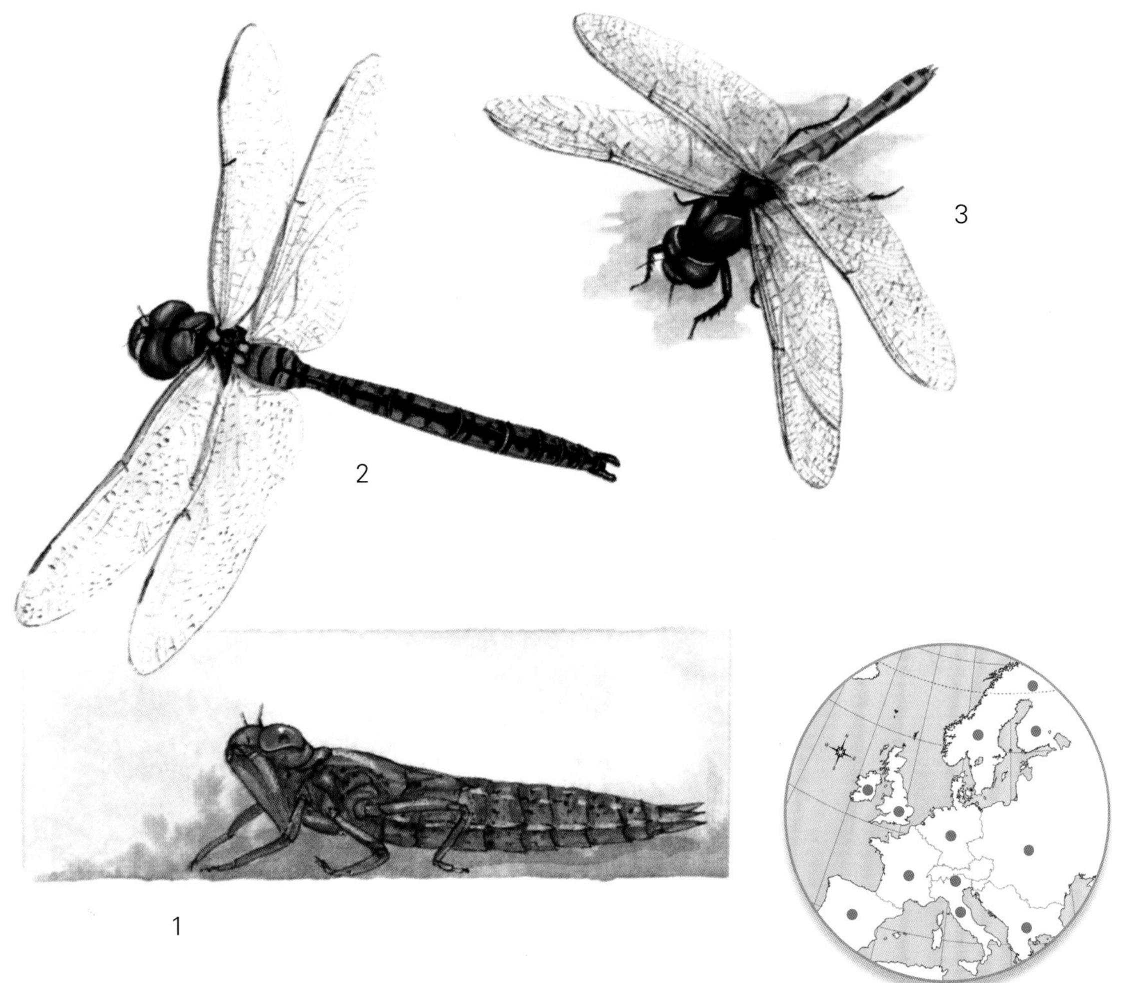
3
2
1

The Emperor Dragonfly can fly long distances and often patrols a specific route.

Damselflies

17 species in Britain

Length: 30–50 mm; wingspan 45–70 mm

Adult Characteristics

Smaller relatives of dragonflies. They have slender bodies and two pairs of large membranous wings with complex veins and cross veins. When at rest they hold their wings together over their back. They have large heads and eyes like dragonflies.

Adult Biology

Adults live near water. They spend much of their time resting on vegetation, flying out at passing prey (like mosquitoes), and fly mostly in sunshine, with a weak drifting flight.

Larvae Characteristics and Biology

Nymphs (**1**) live in water of ponds and streams, like dragonfly nymphs but can easily be distinguished from them by the three plate-like gills at the tail end of the abdomen. They catch their prey with a mask in the same way as dragonfly nymphs.

Common Species

Broad-Winged Damselflies, like **Demoiselles** (**2**) are large damselflies with broad wings. They are less common than the Narrow-Winged Damselflies, which have wings that are stalked at the base; these include the red and the blue damselflies, like the **Blue-Tailed Damselfly** (**3**).

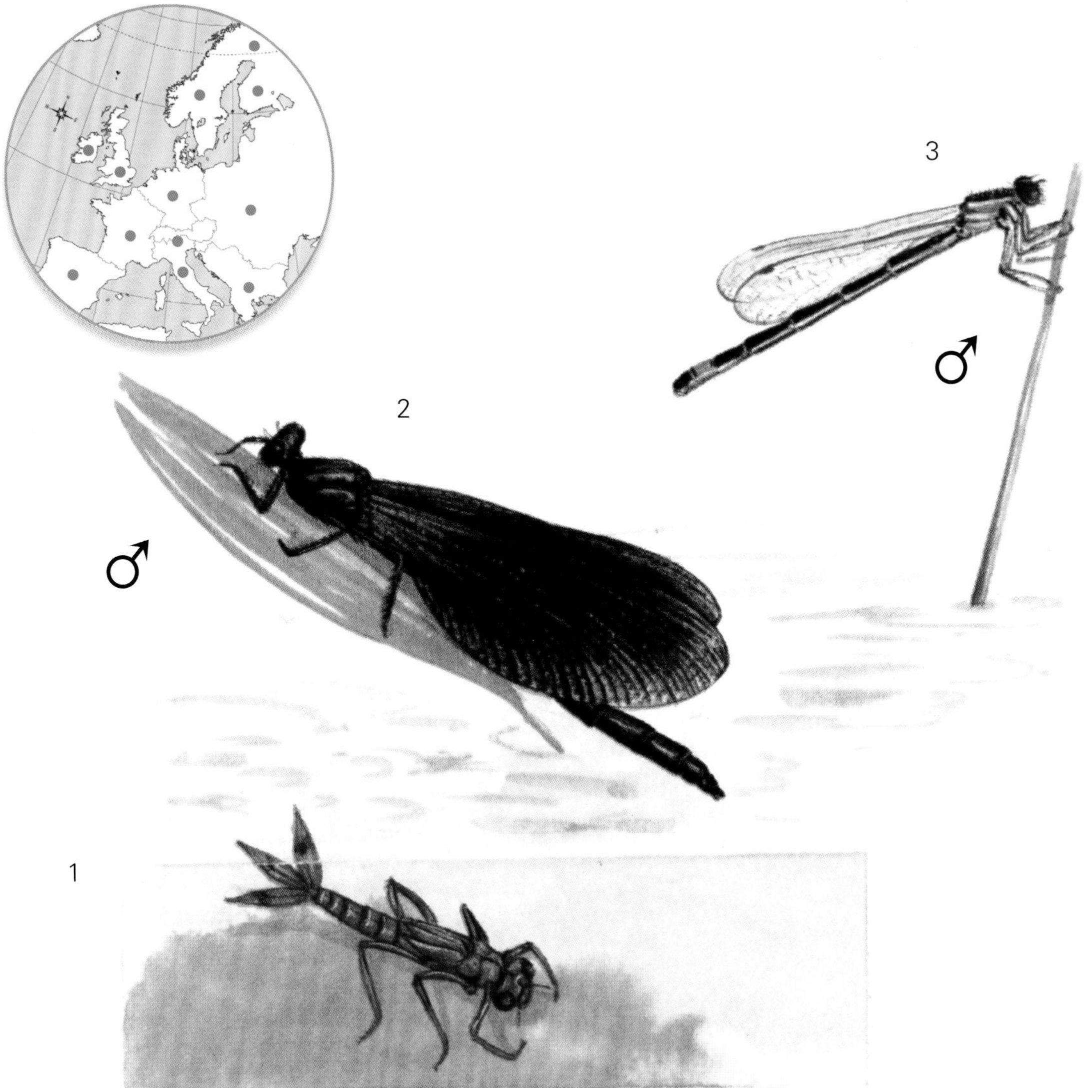
3
♂
2
♂
1

Demoiselles are large damselflies with broad wings. Damselflies are the smaller relatives of dragonflies.

Stoneflies

34 species in Britain

Length: 4–30 mm; wingspan to 50 mm

Adult Characteristics

Medium-sized soft-bodied, flattened insects with two long antennae on head and often with two long tail filaments on abdomen. The two pairs of large membranous wings have many veins. When at rest the wings are folded over the abdomen.

Adult Biology

Stoneflies are most common near running water, especially chalk and mountain streams. Adults are poor fliers and often found under stones, on tree trunks or resting on vegetation near water.

Larvae Characteristics and Biology

Nymphs (**1**) resemble smaller wingless adults, some with tufted gills on thorax and abdomen. They live under stones or debris, in streams with clean, unpolluted, usually fast-flowing, well-oxygenated water. They have two long abdominal tail filaments.

Common Species

There are two similar large species known as **Large Stoneflies** (**2**), both found near stony rivers. Needle Flies are generally smaller and rest with the wings rolled around the sides of their bodies. The February Red is unusual in living near muddy streams and rivers and in flying in late winter and early spring.

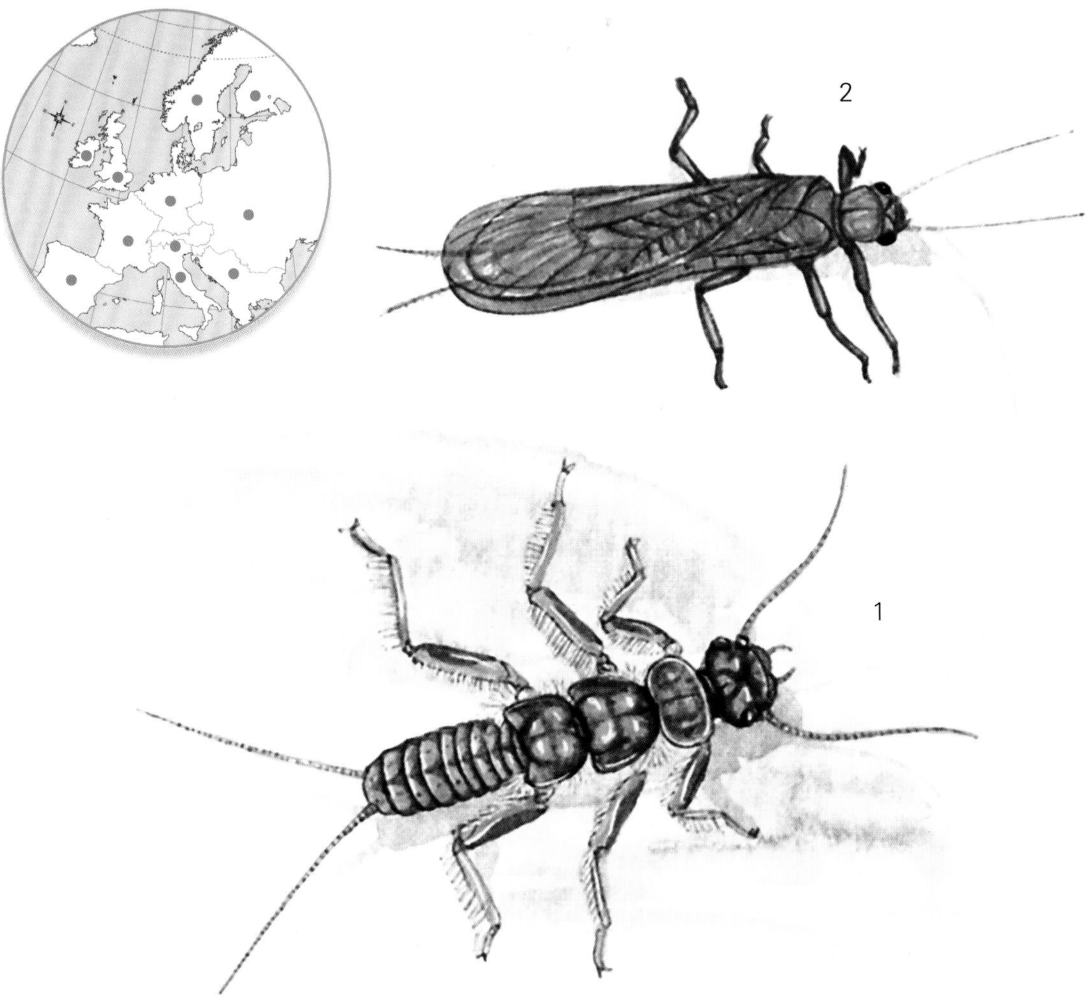
2
1

Mayflies

46 species in Britain

Length: up to 25 mm

Adult Characteristics

Insects with soft brownish or yellowish bodies and two or three long tail filaments. Most have two pairs of wings, held erect when insect is resting. Fore wings large, more or less triangular with many veins and cross veins; hind wings smaller or absent.

Adult Biology

Found near water. Nymphs emerge from water to become immature adults, moulting to become adults within 48 hours. Live for a few days or less. Flight weak. Males gather in swarms.

Larvae Characteristics and Biology

Nymphs (**1**) live in lakes and rivers, in bottom mud, under stones, in moss or crevices on the banks. Up to 25 mm long, they have abdominal gills and three long tail filaments. They emerge in summer from the water to become adults.

Common Species

Common burrowing mayflies, like the **Green Drake** (**2**), grow up to 25 mm long. Most species are smaller than this, up to 12 mm long. All are found near slow-moving rivers or ponds where the nymphs live. Stream mayflies live near streams where their nymphs hide under stones in fast-flowing water.

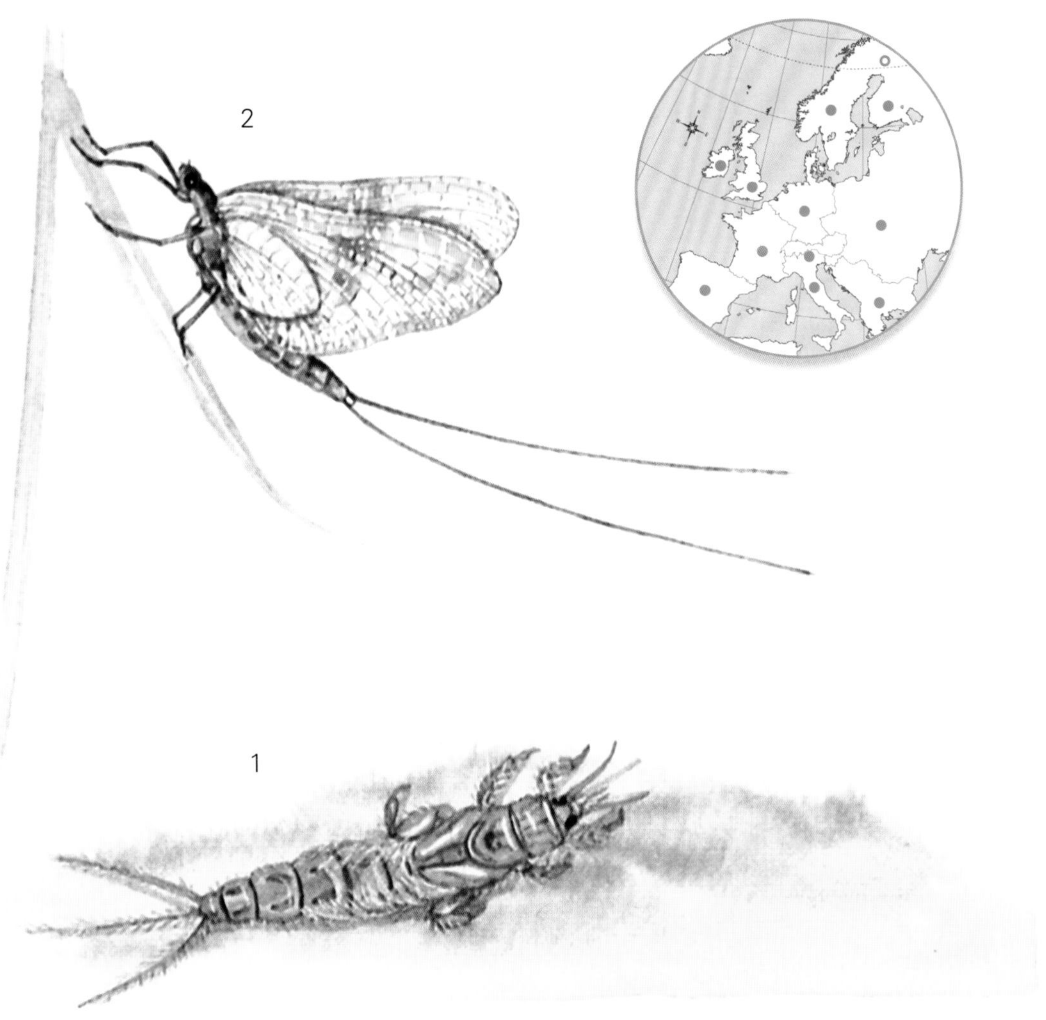
2
1

Earwigs

4 species in Britain

Length: 5–30 mm

Adult Characteristics

Elongated, flattened, leathery, brown or black insects with characteristic forceps at end of abdomen. Antennae about half the length of the body. Some are wingless, most have short hard fore wings that cover the folded membranous hind wings.

Adult Biology

Live in damp places, crevices, under bark or in soil, hiding by day and emerging at night. They are omnivorous. Some are pests in flower gardens.

Larvae Characteristics and Biology

Nymphs (**1**) similar to adults, but often paler and softer and with wing buds that enlarge with each moult. Many live in family groups until they become adults, guarded by mother, in similar places to the adults.

Common Species

Common Earwig (**2**) is the commonest species in Europe and the only common one in Britain; it is often a garden pest. Others are similar in form, but may climb high into trees or shrubs, dig burrows in the ground, live on stream banks or on seashores.

1
♂
2

The Common Earwig rests during the day in damp crevices, but emerges at night to scavenge.

Other Insects

Ant-Lions

About 40 species in Europe, none in Britain. Large insects with long narrow bodies and four delicate, net-veined wings. Wingspan up to 90 mm. Antennae stout and clubbed. Most adults (**1**) fly at night with slow, fluttering flight. They rest by day in vegetation, with wings in roof-like position. Larva (**2**) lives in sandy soil, often buried at the bottom of a pit, seizing with large jaws any insets which fall in. Found in warm, dry areas; *Myrmeleon formicarius* (illustrated) occurs from Scandinavia southwards.

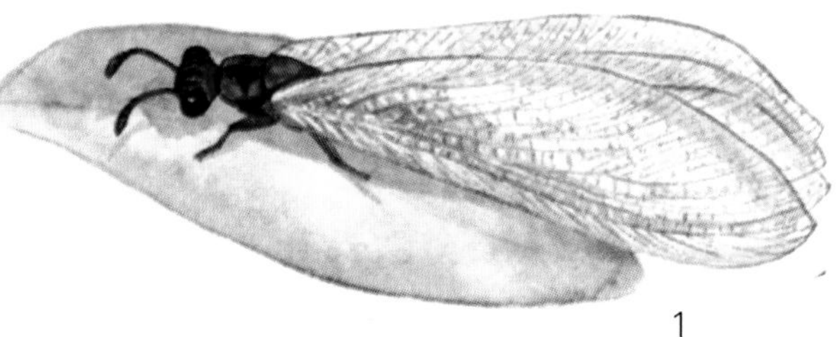

1

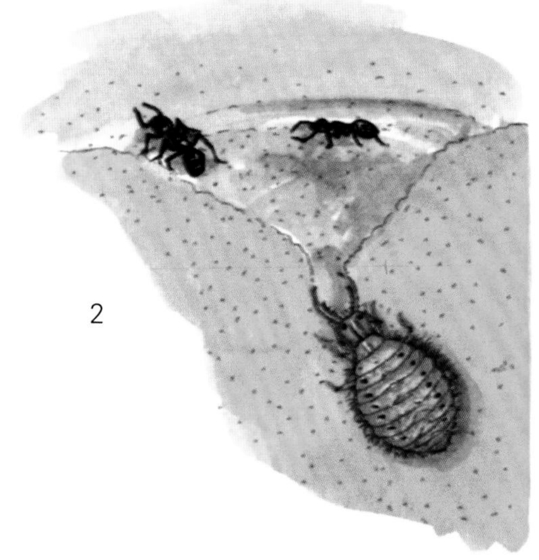

2

Other Insects

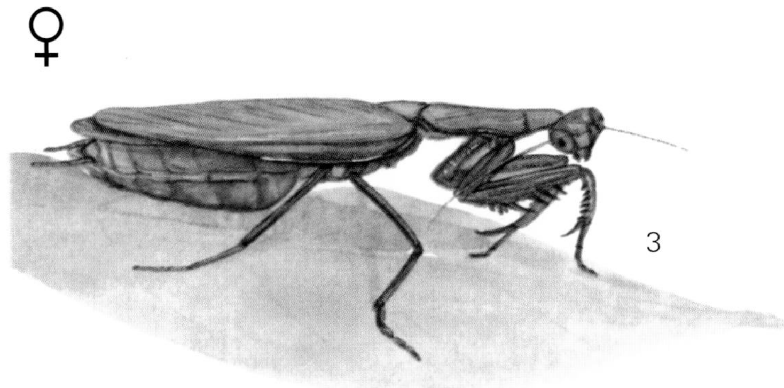

Mantises

About 18 species in Europe, none in Britain. Elongated insects with cylindrical, leathery bodies up to 75 mm long, and long, slender antennae. Usually green or brown. Hind wings membranous, fore wings thickened and cover hind wings when at rest. Front legs very large and modified for catching prey, with spines along inside edge for holding prey. Found on trees and shrubs, motionless or stalking prey. Some are attracted to lights at night. **Praying Mantis** (**3**) is the most common species.

The adult female Praying Mantis usually eats the male after or even during mating.

Other Insects

Alder Flies

Two species in Britain. Medium-sized insects, about 25 mm long, generally smoky brown in colour, with soft bodies and two pairs of delicate, net-veined wings. Antennae long and slender. Veins of wings do not fork at margins. Adult Alder Flies (**1**) fly by day, or rest in vegetation near water. Flight weak and drifting. Larvae (**2**) live in slow-moving or still water. They have three pairs of legs and seven pairs of feathery gills on the abdomen. They crawl onto land to pupate and adults emerge in spring or early summer.

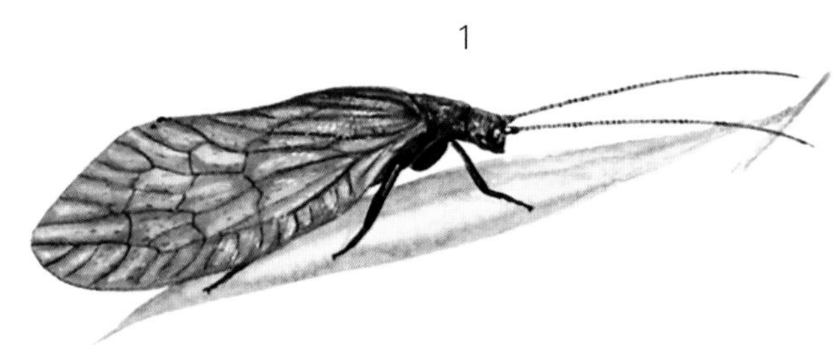

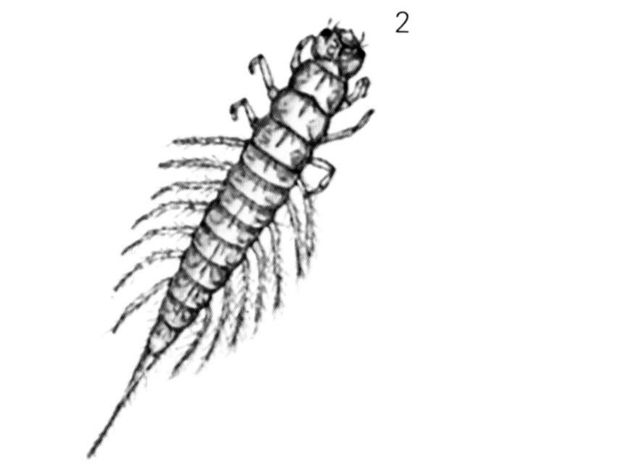

Other Insects

Snake Flies (3)

Four species in Britain. Soft-bodied, brownish insects, with two pairs of net-veined wings (wingspan up to 30 mm). Head carried high above body on long prothorax. Found in woodland or near streams.

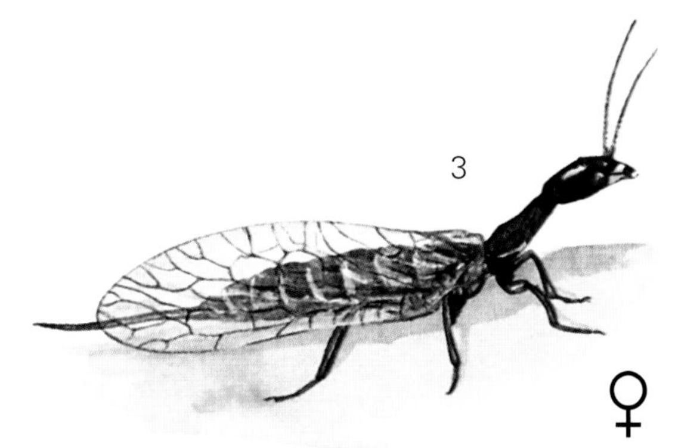

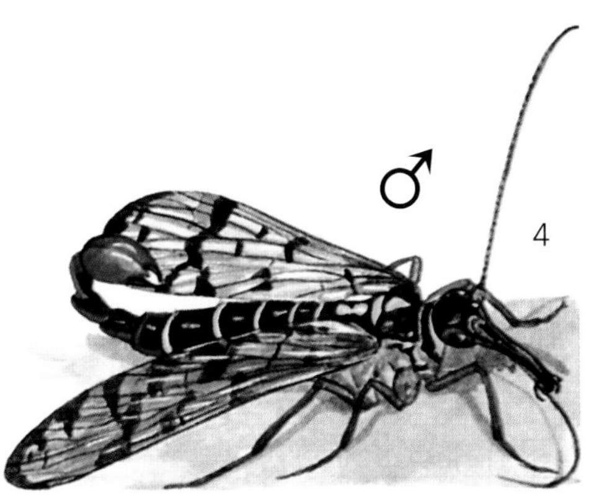

Scorpion Flies (4)

Three species in Britain. Medium-sized insects with two pairs of net-veined, brown-spotted wings. Wingspan 25–30 mm. Some males have a turned-up abdomen like a scorpion's sting. Found in wooded areas. Larvae resemble caterpillars; they live in soil or leaf litter.

Fleas and Lice

Fleas

About 60 species in Britain. Brown or black, wingless insects, flattened from side to side, up to 5 mm long. Most have hard bodies with many spines and bristles. Hind legs are long and used in jumping. Fleas live in nests and lairs of birds and mammals. They include **Cat Fleas** (**1**) and **Human Fleas** (**2**). They suck the blood of their hosts, and may carry diseases like typhus and plague. Rabbit fleas carry myxomatosis. Eggs are laid in debris or dust; larvae feed on hairs and other organic remains.

Fleas and Lice

Sucking Lice

About 25 species in Britain. Wingless, oval or circular, pale, flat-bodied insects, up to 5 mm long. Legs are short and bent inwards, clinging to hair. Parasites on mammals, sucking blood. **Human Head Louse** (**3**) lives on the head.

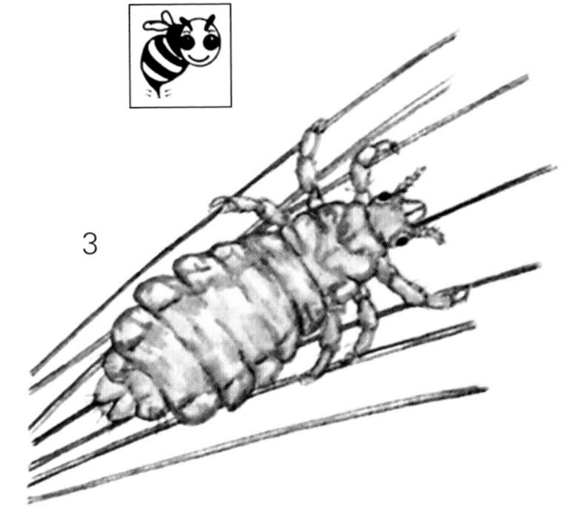

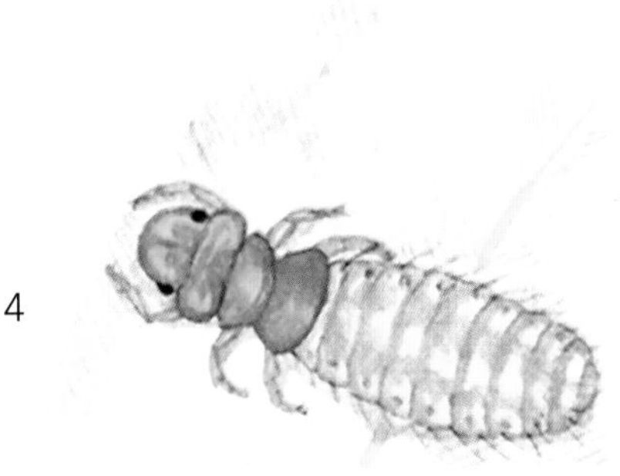

Biting Lice

About 500 species in Britain. Elongated or oval, bristly, wingless insects, up to 5 mm long. Clinging legs small and stout. Parasites on mammals and birds, feeding on feathers, hair, skin or blood. **Shaft Louse** (**4**) lives on chickens.

Springtails

About 300 species in Britain

Length: usually 1–5 mm

Adult Characteristics

Tiny, soft-bodied, wingless, usually elongated insects. They vary in colour, most are white or grey, others are yellow or brown. A tube protrudes from the first abdominal segment and a two-pronged 'tail' is bent under the end of the abdomen.

Adult Biology

Springtails can spring into the air if the flexion of the 'tail' is released. They occur almost everywhere, most often in damp soil, rotting vegetation and leaf litter. Some live on water.

Larvae Characteristics and Biology

Nymphs are just like smaller adults in outward appearance, and they are found with them in similar places.

Common Species

Water Springtails (1) live on the water of ponds and streams. Seashore Springtails among seashore rocks. Many Globular Springtails live in plants, like the **Lucerne Flea (2)** which may be a pest in peas. **Slender Springtails (3)** live in leaf litter, rotting wood, under stones etc.; some are greenhouse pests.

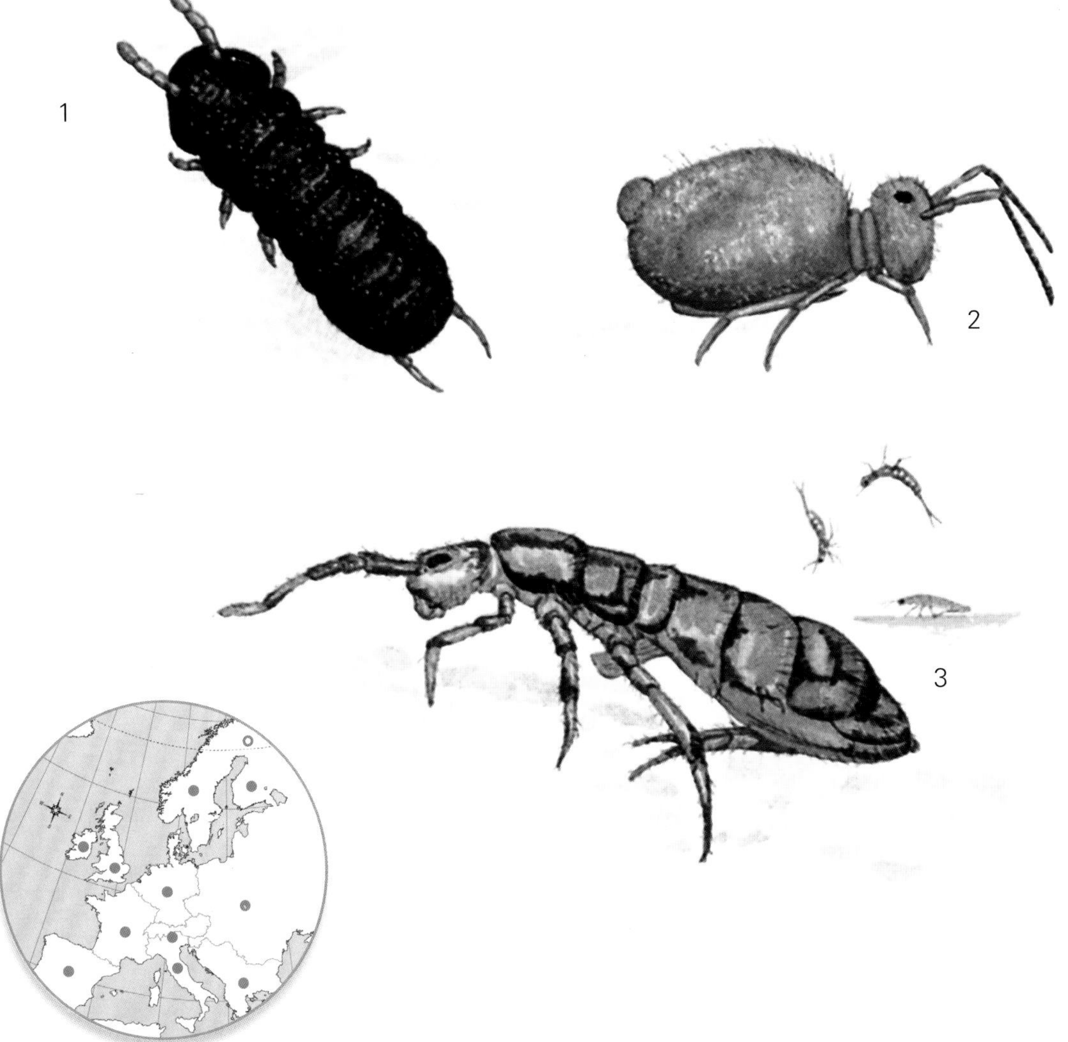
1
2
3

Silverfish and Firebrats

Length: 7–12 mm

2 species in Britain

Adult Characteristics

Soft, flattened, wingless insects, brown or silver-grey in colour and covered in scales. They have three long tail filaments on the abdomen and two long antennae on the head. Eyes are small and wide apart.

Adult Biology

Found in houses; these insects run quickly into hiding if disturbed. Silverfish feed on dried starchy foods, book bindings and paper glue. Firebrats eat kitchen scraps.

Larvae Characteristics and Biology

Nymphs are similar to adults and have a similar lifestyle. They take about two years to mature.

Common Species

Silverfish (1) are covered with tiny silver scales; they live in cupboards, in bathrooms, behind bookcases. **Firebrats (2)** are brown and grey; they live in warm places, near boilers and heating pipes. Other related bristletails live in soil, leaf litter, rotting wood and caves; also on the seashore.

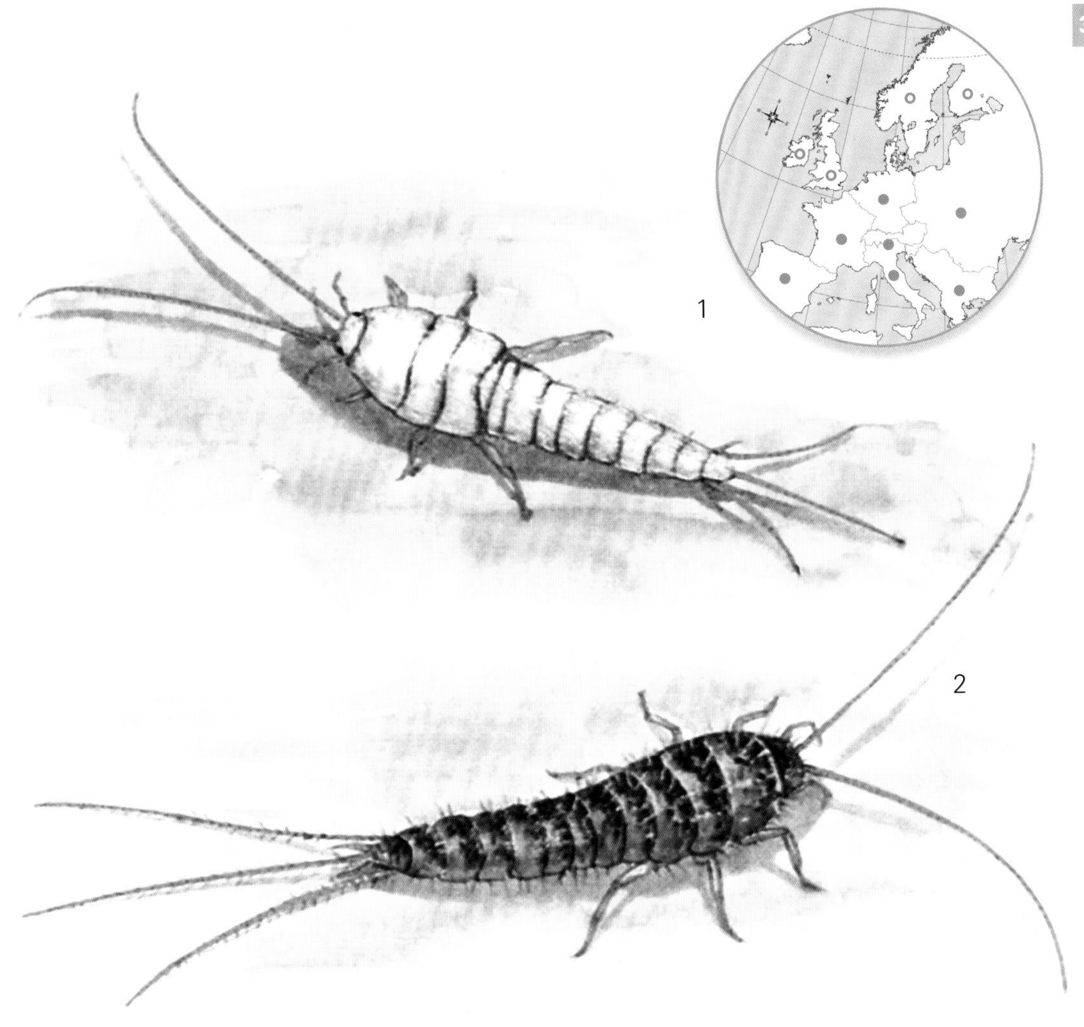
1
2

Further Reading

Asher, J. (ed) et al, *The Millennium Atlas of Butterflies in Britain and Ireland*, Oxford University Press, 2001

Brooks, S. (ed), *Field Guide to the Dragonflies and Damselflies of Great Britain and Ireland*, British Wildlife Publishing, 1997

Chapman, R.F., *The Insects: Structure and Function*, Cambridge University Press, 1998

Chinery, M., *Collins Complete British Insects*, Collins, 2005

Chinery, M., *Field Guide to the Insects of Britain and Northern Europe*, Collins, 1993

Eisener, T. and M., *Secret Weapons: Defenses of Insects, Spiders, Scorpions, and Other Many-Legged Creatures*, The Belknap Press, 2005

Eisner, T., *For Love of Insects*, The Belknap Press, 2005

Evans, A.V. and Bellamy, C.L., *An Inordinate Fondness for Beetles*, University of California Press, 2000

Field Guide to the Butterflies and Other Insects of Britain, Reader's Digest, 2001

Grimaldi, D. and Engel, M.S., *Evolution of the Insects*, Cambridge University Press, 2005

Gullan, P.J., *Insects: An Outline of Entomology*, Blackwell Publishing, 2004

Marshall, J.A. and Haes, C., *Grasshoppers and Allied Insects of Great Britain and Ireland*, Harley Books, 1990

McGavin, G., *Insects (Pocket Nature)*, Dorling Kindersley Publishers Ltd., 2005

McGavin, M., *Essential Entomology: An Order-By-Order Introduction*, Oxford University Press, 2001

Merian, M.S., *Flowers, Butterflies and Insects*, Dover Publications Inc., 1991

Olsen, L., *Small Woodland Creatures*, Oxford University Press, 2001

Resh, V.H. (ed) and Carde, R.T., *Encyclopedia of Insects*, Academic Press Inc., 2003

Roberts, M.J., *Spiders of Britain and Northern Europe*, Collins, 2001

Skinner, G.J., *Ants of the British Isles*, Shire Publications Ltd., 1987

Waring, T. and Townsend, M., *Field Guide to the Moths of Great Britain and Ireland*, British Wildlife Publishing, 2003

Picture Credits

All photographs courtesy of NHPA/Photoshot: Anthony Bannister: 258–9; Alan Barnes: 24–5, 50–1, 58–9; Simon Booth: 20–1, 264–5; N.A. Callow: 106–7, 120–1, 148–9, 168–9, 174–5, 200–1, 206–7, 222–3, 234–5, 268–9; Gerry Cambridge: 32–3; Laurie Campbell: 40–1, 44–5, 54–5, 68–9, 82–3, 188–9, 192–3; Bill Coster: 250–1; Stephen Dalton: 90–1, 124–5, 132–3, 154–5, 162–3, 182–3, 214–5, 230–1, 240–1, 246–7, 282–3, 306–7, 322–3; Susanne Danegger: 310–1; Guy Edwardes: 316–7; Ron Fotheringham: 334–5; Martin Garwood: 64–5, 72–3, 114–5, 142–3, 210–1, 226–7; Martin Harvey: 254–5; Daniel Heuclin: 338–9; Ernie Janes: 102–3, 278–9; Mike Lane: 326–7; John Shaw: 110–1; Robert Thompson: 28–9, 36–7, 76–7; Martin Wendler: 302–3.

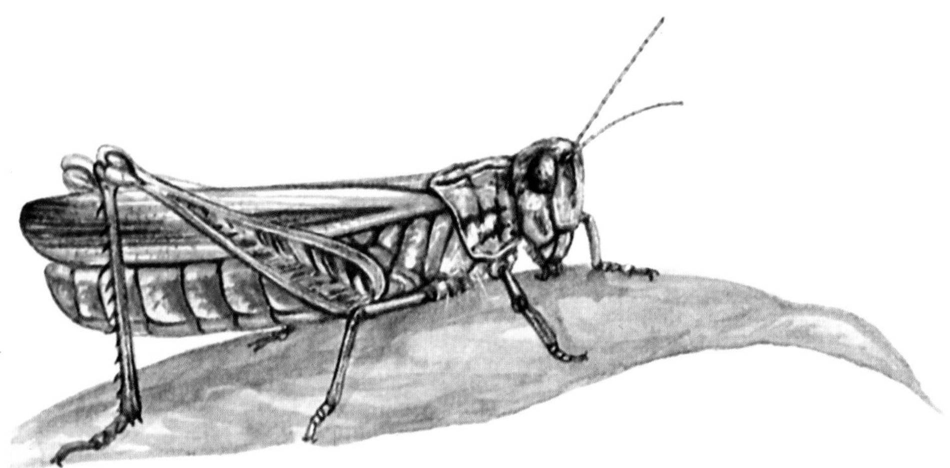

Index and Checklist

Keep a record of your sightings by ticking the boxes.